ADVANCE PRAISE FOR

"I have long believed that left to their own devices generate all of our struggles in the workplace. The flip side to this is that our mindsets and expectations alone allow us to find joy and success at work, *and* that with the right tools we can even find that success and happiness are our natural states, once the drama is gone. *Zen Your Work* is a powerful collection of those tools that will teach you how to navigate the most pressing challenges you'll face in the office with a fresh set of eyes."

—Cy Wakeman, author of *No Ego* and *Reality-Based Leadership*

"Karlyn offers a foundational and practical approach to self-awareness in the workplace, so we can stay zen and take ownership of our mental health regardless of our circumstances at work. She shows us how to set the right tone in leadership and communication to create a productive path forward to success."

—John Baldino, president of Humareso

"*Zen Your Work* is a fantastic toolkit for anyone who wants to create the most meaningful work experience possible, regardless of their coworkers' moods, organizational change, and other external circumstances. The book will help you understand your strengths and biases so that you can enjoy smoother, less stressful interactions and greater success."

—Alice Boyes, PhD, author of *The Healthy Mind Toolkit*

"*Zen Your Work* is a wonderful book for coping with everyone at work, including high-conflict personalities. From how to start your day well, to the stories you tell yourself on-the-job, to building strategic relationships, Dr. Borysenko gives lots of tools and tips for finding and creating your ideal work situation. After reading this book, you'll know how to thrive (not just survive) regardless of what everyone else does. Surprisingly simple, clear, and friendly."

—Bill Eddy, author of *5 Types of People Who Can Ruin Your Life*

zen your work

CREATE YOUR IDEAL
WORK EXPERIENCE THROUGH
MINDFUL SELF-MASTERY

Karlyn Borysenko,
MBA, PhD

A TarcherPerigee Book

tarcherperigee

An imprint of Penguin Random House LLC
375 Hudson Street
New York, New York 10014

Most TarcherPerigee books are available at special quantity discounts for bulk purchase for sales promotions, premiums, fund-raising, and educational needs. Special books or book excerpts also can be created to fit specific needs. For details, write: SpecialMarkets@penguinrandomhouse.com.

Library of Congress Cataloging-in-Publication Data

Names: Borysenko, Karlyn, author.
Title: Zen your work : create your ideal work experience through mindful
    self-mastery / Karlyn Borysenko, MBA, PhD.
Description: New York : TarcherPerigee, 2018. |
Identifiers: LCCN 2018016224 (print) | LCCN 2018016959 (ebook) |
    ISBN 9780525505198 (e-book) | ISBN 9780143133391 (pbk.)
Subjects: LCSH: Employee morale. | Employee motivation. | Work—
    Psychological aspects. | Employees—Attitudes.
Classification: LCC HF5549.5.M6 (ebook) | LCC HF5549.5.M6 B67 2018
    (print) | DDC 650.1—dc23
LC record available at https://lccn.loc.gov/2018016224

Printed in the United States of America
1   3   5   7   9   10   8   6   4   2

Book design by Daniel Lagin

CONTENTS

Introduction

Anyone who has spent time in the professional world has probably had a less-than-ideal work experience (or several), and I am no exception. But one of my jobs was particularly bad. The organization was like a magnet for some of the most toxic individuals I've ever encountered—cynics, pessimists, and downright narcissists were in almost all the leadership positions, and their attitudes permeated the rest of the staff. My best days there were the ones when I just sat at my desk, stared at my computer, and didn't say anything to anyone at all. But with a calendar full of meetings, that was rarely an option.

When I did interact with my coworkers, everything was a fight, every project was a struggle, and nothing was ever good enough. I was underutilized, unappreciated, and spent my car rides home each evening either crying or yelling at the universe for putting me in this situation.

But even the most horrible things we experience can be a blessing. This is the position that taught me what it means to zen your work. During a particularly toxic time, I made one of the best decisions I could have—getting the heck out of Dodge to go on a weeklong cruise in the Caribbean. Stuck in the middle of the ocean with no internet access (who wants to pay the wifi rates on a cruise!), I had time to reflect on how I had created this situation for myself, and what I needed to do to get out of it.

When you zen your work, you embrace the concept that you are in control of your professional experience and mindful of how everything you do creates it. Most people are quick to abdicate responsibility, but great work experiences don't just magically appear out of thin air. They are created by people who are determined to make the choices that support the vision they have for themselves. It's everything from how you approach an individual task, to the way you interact with your coworkers, to the attitude and perspective that you bring with you to the office every day.

What I realized was that I couldn't control the other people in the organization, but I could control myself, my perspective, and my actions. That meant that even on the worst days, I could get a win because I could set the standard for what a win was. I wrote a mantra for myself that became my benchmark for success:

> *Act with integrity,*
> *have compassion and empathy (even when others don't),*
> *and be of service to people around you.*

If I achieved those three things, I considered it a good day. Nothing else mattered—not my boss throwing me under the bus or my coworker spreading gossip. Everything involved in meeting my standard was my form of zen. It was that laser-focus on what I could control that made the difference because as long as I had good days, all the nonsense didn't matter so much. And because I reduced my stress, I had enough energy left over to plan my escape route so that I could leave the toxic job and create the professional experience I wanted.

Zen Your Work will guide you through the process I discovered during my journey in a way that will empower anyone in any position—from entry level to executive—to create their ideal professional experience from the inside out. It's a guide to bridging the gap between where you are now and what will allow you to achieve the most professional happiness and success. Self-mastery is our goal—the art of accepting responsibility, understanding your innate working style, and discerning when and how to push outside of your comfort zone. You'll get there by learning to apply mindfulness techniques in a highly practical way to achieve your professional ambitions, create game-changing relationships (even with the most negative people in the office), decrease your stress, and enjoy improved work-life balance. This book isn't a recitation of academic studies—everything in it has been applied and tested in the real world. In my work today as an organizational psychologist and coach, I've used these techniques with young professionals just out of college, mid-career professionals looking for that next big promotion, and seasoned executives who have tried all the "traditional" strategies. In every scenario, they've been able to take these ideas, apply them immediately, and experience results.

The people who've made these techniques work for them are no different from you. They're not smarter, more driven, or more disciplined. They're just people, full of their own blend of strengths and glorious flaws. They simply put in the work to make their ideal work experience a reality. There's no trick to this . . . but there's no shortcut either. Think of it as training for a marathon. No one can do that work for you—if you don't show up and put in the miles, you'll have a hard time finishing the race.

So if creating a happy, fulfilling experience is something you want, make the decision right now to show up. The rest of this book will guide you on the path to get there.

PART I

know
yourself

When you zen your work, you commit to discovering and embracing the choices that will lead to the experience you want. You don't need others to create an amazing work experience for you, but you do need to get your head in order. Doing that requires a new understanding of who you are, the unconscious choices you make, and what you express to the world (and to your coworkers) every day.

In this section, you'll go more in-depth about what it means to zen your work, learn to take control of your work day, and gain new mastery of yourself and your innate work style.

CHAPTER 1

Zen Your Work

Peace cannot be kept by force. It can only be achieved by
understanding.

—**Albert Einstein**

GOAL FOR THIS CHAPTER:

Learn what it means to zen your work, and understand the structure of the rest of the book.

We all have those days when you wake up and the very
first thing you think is "This day is going to suck!"
After hitting snooze a few times, trying to avoid the
inevitable, you drag yourself out from under the covers and mope
around miserably while getting ready for work. On the commute
in, you visualize all the things you're dreading when you arrive at
work, playing them out in your head as if the worst-case scenario is

the most probable outcome of all the meetings and interactions with your coworkers you'll experience throughout the day. You "know" your coworkers are out to get you and your boss is going to try to throw you under the bus—there's nothing you can do to stop it. So, before you've even arrived and had your first cup of coffee (or maybe your second if you're really lucky!), you've worked yourself into a tizzy. Your whole body is tense and you can feel your stress levels brimming over already. Nothing has even happened yet and you're ready to go to battle.

Now let's examine an alternative: You wake up, notice the sun beaming in through the window, and think, "It looks like it's going to be a beautiful day!" You lie in a bed for a few minutes and listen to the birds chirping outside before plunging into your morning routine. While you're getting ready, you think about the things you want to get accomplished today, and begin to map out what it will take to hit your goals. On the way into the office, you sing along to some of your favorite music in the car, where it doesn't matter if you have a less-than-perfect voice because you're just having fun. You get to work, drop your things at your desk, and head to the kitchen to grab your cup of coffee, greeting your coworkers in the hall on your way there with a smile.

Here's the thing: Each of these realities is possible every single morning. Which one would you prefer? Which one sets you up for success? Which one will make you the happiest? It's your choice to make.

You see, the world is a perfect place. It's not perfect in the sense that we get what we want the minute we want it, or that things always work out in what we perceive to be a fair and just way—it's perfect in that we get exactly what we should expect to get based on our actions and contributions to every situation. If we aren't taking individual responsibility or vocalizing the need for change when things aren't going in the direction we want them to go, then we shouldn't expect that things are going to change course. This is true of the big things (who our president is, the existence of war, the state of human rights), and it's true of the day-to-day challenges you face in and out of your professional environment.

When it comes to work, both our good days and our bad days start before we ever make it to the office or encounter a single person. Without a drastic change in perspective, is there any chance the person in our first example is going to be able to turn it around and have an amazing, productive, fulfilling day? Probably not. Everything they've done so far has set them up to fail. Yet if they have a bad day, they will find a way to make it everyone else's fault—their boss's, their colleagues', their team's. This person is coming into the office looking for things to go wrong, and they will probably be successful at it. It's very easy to find things we don't like in projects, meetings, or other people when we're specifically looking for them.

Now, don't get me wrong—person number two in our example isn't assured a perfect day just because they had a better morning than person number one, but they've set themselves on a much better path. They've put themselves in a good mood, thought about their goals, and cultivated a relationship with their coworkers, all before their first cup of coffee! And when things start to go off the rails (as they inevitably will at work), we can already guess that, given a choice, this is a person who will look for the best path around any obstacles that come up rather than complain when things aren't going their way. They're in control, and they know that their experience is dependent upon their perspective and their actions.

In her book *Broadcasting Happiness*, positive psychology researcher Michelle Gielan notes that "the stories we tell about the world predict whether we believe that happiness is a choice and whether we'll take action to create happiness—or stay stagnant, inert, and powerless." In other words, saying we want to be happy at work is one thing. Doing the things required to make it happen is quite another. Happiness, success, productivity . . . all those things are choices that play out in the little things we do every moment of every day, beginning with the perspective that we bring to each and every situation.

As a tangible example of how this works, think about losing weight. It's easy to say, "I want to lose weight," but if you don't really believe you can lose weight, your actions probably won't align with what you need to do to burn those extra calories. We all know someone who has struggled with their weight—who says that they would love to lose a few pounds but they feel like they've "tried everything" and nothing has worked. That mindset that "nothing works" is the nail in their weight-loss coffin because no one can lose weight for you (except maybe a plastic surgeon). If you don't drink lots of water, watch what you eat, and work out, chances are that scale won't move much. Doing all those things requires sacrifice— giving up your nightly dessert and sugary drinks that you might be addicted to and getting up early to hit the gym. Sacrifice can be painful, so we don't do it if we don't believe it will get us to a greater goal. But if you believe that the sacrifice is worth it and the goal is something you value, that's when your actions will follow suit. Your results will be the sum total of your actions—you'll lose weight!

Work is no different. No one can make you happy or successful at work if you don't first make the decision to do it yourself. It all starts with your mindset and perspective. We just think it's different because there are more people involved, so we have more people to blame when things are going wrong . . . and some of those people have the power to make decisions about how we spend our time (or if we have a job there at all!). But as we saw in the two scenarios at the opening of this chapter, it's a choice that starts the moment you wake up every morning. Do you want to come home from work miserable every single day, blaming other people for your state of affairs? Or do you want to create an amazing, fulfilling, productive work experience for yourself, regardless of what anyone around you says or does?

If you're still with me, I'm going to assume you chose the latter option—an amazing, fulfilling, productive work experience . . . whatever that means to you! Good! But saying it is the easy part. Doing it is where the real work begins.

That's what we'll cover in the remainder of this book—strategies that you can use every day to support the perspective and actions you need to create the work experience you want. And because perspective is so important, I've not only grounded this work in psychology, but also in mindfulness techniques to help you zen your work. Mindfulness has existed for thousands of years all over the world as a way for human beings to navigate their experiences without getting caught up in negativity, fear, anxiety, anger, or self-doubt.

WHAT IT MEANS TO ZEN YOUR WORK

When I was working on my PhD in industrial/organizational psychology, I founded my practice Zen Workplace. With a name like that, you can imagine that organizations come to me all the time looking for help in integrating mindfulness strategies into their employee experience. The first thing I always ask them is "What do you mean by mindfulness?" And I'll get a different answer from each person. It's one of those buzzwords that means different things to different people based on when and how they originally encountered the concept. So before we get too far, let's make sure we're on the same page and are working with a common definition.

People who are mindful (and are thus able to zen their work successfully) are nonjudgmentally aware of what's going on in the present moment. There are three parts to this:

Be aware

This is about being fully conscious of what is going on in your mind, your body, and your surroundings in the current situation. For example, say you're in a meeting. What are you thinking? How do you feel about it? What excites you? What are you afraid of? How does your body feel? Are you tense and constricted, or loose and flexible? Who else is there? What do they need? How can you help them? Most people shut down in a meeting, simply wanting it to be over, or waiting for their turn to talk instead of listening. But being aware of the internal and external factors involved can help you to navigate the meeting more effectively, getting you closer to your goals.

Be nonjudgmental

We love to classify things as good or bad, right or wrong, better or worse. Most of the time, we default to focusing on things we perceive as negative. This is evolutionary. Think back to when we were cavemen and were out gathering food. The bushes twenty feet away from us start to rustle. Why? Is it the wind? Or is it an animal that has come to eat us? If we don't default to assuming the worst and run away, we might not have a second chance to do it!

But unless you're a zookeeper, you're not in danger of getting eaten at work these days. Most of the time, things just are—they're not good or bad, black or white. We are the ones who create the stories in our heads that provide the context for judgment. If you look at things nonjudgmentally, you can use that grounding to create the story that best serves you. For example, if you don't get the budget you were hoping for, you might have a knee-jerk reaction to that: "Now I'll never meet my goals. They obviously don't want me to succeed." Instead, reserve that judgment, and you'll be able to see other outcomes and possibilities. You don't have the budget to do your project—that's our nonjudgmental reality. Maybe that frees you up to take on a new project, or maybe you can refine your original idea and make it even better to argue for the budget again later. Those are two distinct possibilities that could result in better outcomes, but you only got there by looking at it as if you were looking at pieces on a chessboard and figuring out the best next move. The more you can reserve judgment, the more effectively you'll be able to navigate toward your desired outcome.

Be present

Most of our anxieties come from things that have happened to us in the past. We learned that work must be hard because we watched our parents come home miserable every day, or that our bosses are to be feared because we've had bad ones before, or that our coworkers are only looking out for themselves instead of for the good of the team. When you let past interactions and outcomes influence how you perceive things going on in the present, you might find yourself focusing on the most negative possible outcome to your current situation. Instead, let the past be simply that—the past. It happened and there's nothing you can do to change it, but that doesn't mean you're doomed to repeat it. Simply make the decision to actively prevent it from influencing your present moment. That allows you to focus on what's right in front of you, right now, in a beautifully detached manner that will lead you to make better decisions.

Let's be honest—most of your common day-to-day experiences at work are probably anything but zen-like! Most people are in a constant reactive state, running from meeting to meeting, doing things the boss wants on a whim, responding to requests from co-workers or subordinates, barely finding any time to work on their own tasks during the day without being interrupted with an email or phone call, and working much later than five p.m. to meet deadlines and goals. When you zen your work by being aware, nonjudgmental, and present, you'll take proactive control of your experience by taking back the power you've given others to impact your day. This is about holding yourself accountable to create a positive work experience, understanding that no one can inflict a negative experience on you if you refuse to buy into it.

IT'S MORE THAN MEDITATION

When some people use the word *mindfulness*, meditation comes instantly to mind. In fact, many people use the words interchangeably. Now, I'm a big fan of meditation. I meditate for at least thirty minutes almost every single day, and when I don't do it, I feel as though I'm not at my best. I also believe that meditation is your ultimate shortcut to embracing the perspective you need to get the most from the strategies in this book. It will teach you to be aware and fully present in every situation, help you to clear your head so you get out of your own way, and release resistance to the ideas that you find most challenging. If that's something you're interested in, there are a ton of books, articles, and blog posts on meditation, and even free guided meditations on Spotify and YouTube to get you started. There's no "right" way to start a meditation practice. Don't get bogged down in the "shoulds"—just start doing it!

However, I want to be crystal clear: You do not have to maintain a meditation practice to embrace the strategies in this book, and that's why I'm not going to cover meditation specifically. It is a shortcut, but it is not the only path. Remember, we're being non-judgmental here. Meditation is great for some people. But others have a really tough time with it or are simply not inclined to try. That's okay too! Whatever path you're on, this book will help you make progress toward creating your ideal professional experience.

SPOILER ALERT: THIS IS NOT EASY

I am absolutely useless before I have a cup of coffee in the morning. If you ever see me at a conference before nine a.m. and I don't have a Starbucks venti quad soy vanilla latte in my hand, just wait until later to approach me. Trust me, you will have my undying appreciation and you'll get much more of my attention and focus after I have had my caffeine injection. And I make sure that people know this about me. We all have our boundaries and this one is mine.

I share this factoid as context for this story: I once had a boss report me to human resources because I walked by her office one morning and didn't say hello after she said good morning to me. Hand to God, I don't remember this ever happening (and if it did, it was because I was on my way to the kitchen to get my cup of coffee), but she was adamant that it was clear evidence that I was giving her the silent treatment.

It was with this gem of a boss that I first started utilizing the techniques in this book. It was not an ideal situation. I was in a job I hated. I didn't trust my coworkers at all. And if you think my boss sounds like a nightmare, her boss (the CEO of the organization) was even worse! I didn't start doing this zen stuff because it was the easy way to gloss over things and pretend all was well. I started doing it because I desperately needed a way to relieve my stress levels so that I could plan my exit from the organization. Fast-forward several years, and as I spend my days teaching others how to do this, there are still moments when it's really hard for me. I have bad days when I find it difficult to get perspective, but I am blessed to have people around me who help me get back on track quickly.

I think it's easy for people who write books about happiness, mindset, positive psychology, or career success to make it all sound easy. Then you try it, find out it's not easy, don't see results right away, and get frustrated and give up. I want you to go into this with your eyes wide open. This. Is. Hard. Making the choice to do the day-to-day work to integrate these techniques into your profes-sional experience is incredibly challenging because it will take you outside of your comfort zone. That's why most people don't do it. It involves a highly disciplined form of detachment where you have to take your ego, wrap it up in a little box, and put it on the shelf for safekeeping. You're going to have to do things to placate people you don't like and to be the voice of reason in emotionally charged situations. None of that is easy.

There are a lot of things going on here. First, you're changing your own habits. You know that intense soreness that happens when you first go back to the gym after a long break from working out? You'll experience that here too—absolute mental soreness. It's hard. It's exhausting. You're going to want to quit because doing things the way you've always done them before is going to be easier than taking the road less traveled!

You're also going to be fighting against decades of life experience telling you to do things the way people around you have always done them, especially your parents (and most of our parents were horrible examples in this regard, going to jobs they hated every day!). You're going to be doing this in the midst of coworkers who are committed to a more cynical approach, and who won't always understand why you're doing things the way you are. People who are miserable want other people around them to be miserable and will do everything they can to drag you down with them. Sometimes the most cynical people are also the loudest and most powerful in the organization, making them even more difficult to ignore.

And you will make mistakes. You will have days when being aware, nonjudgmental, and present is simply not possible. But the emotions you're feeling during those times are temporary and once they pass, you can always come back to the present and leave them behind you—every moment is a chance to begin again. As soon as you make a misstep, poof! There's no beating yourself up. Your mistake is gone and it's a chance to try again.

Stick with it and it will get easier. Consistency and perseverance are key, and the payoff is huge. You will be happier, more productive, more fulfilled, and ultimately more successful. Most of you will be able to stay in your current organization and create a better experience for yourself there. Some of you will have to leave for greener pastures, just like I did. Regardless, you'll experience some temporary pain as you acclimate to the new way of doing things for a career that you can love for the years or decades until you retire. Seems like a pretty good deal!

HOW THIS BOOK WORKS

With our definition and fair warning of what you're getting into out of the way, let's turn our attention to the path forward. This book will guide you through the process of creating your ideal work experience from the inside out.

In Part I: Know Yourself, you'll look inward to understand and accept the unique strengths you bring to work with you. People are incredibly hard on themselves, and it can be easy to forget that you already have everything you need to be successful. You just need to learn to utilize it and empower yourself in the right way.

In Part II: Own Your Perspective, you'll also learn to take control of your perspective in almost any situation at work, removing your ego from the process to see the best next steps with clear eyes.

In Part III: Interacting with Others, you'll learn how to take everything you learned about yourself and your approach in parts I and II and apply it to your interactions with others at work. You'll discover how to build amazing relationships with your coworkers (even the most difficult of the bunch) in order to be able to exert influence outside of your own branch of the organizational chart. We'll work on developing a confident approach to give the people around you the security of knowing that they can trust you and are taken care of in any situation.

And finally, Part IV: Refine Your Path Forward, is a little different. Because once you've used the techniques in the first two parts for a while, you're going to have a different perspective on the job than when you first accepted it. You'll also have a newfound sense of value that you didn't have before. It's worth stepping back and looking at your situation with a fresh set of eyes to consider if your career is on the right track, and what type of boundaries you need to set to create the life experience you want inside and outside of the office.

Just like this introductory chapter, each subsequent chapter will have a goal at the top to give you a quick hit of information about what you can expect to get out of the chapter. I'll also offer exercises along the way to help you enhance your self-mastery, and I'll recommend you have a journal ready to record your notes and document your experiences. Though you can skip around to the sections you feel would be most beneficial, this book is designed to be read and completed sequentially for the greatest impact, at least on your first time through.

Finally, remember that the work you'll be doing will take you outside of your comfort zone. That means that if you're doing it right, it should make you feel uncomfortable. Embrace that feeling—learn to love it and consider it an indicator that you're making progress. The more you do, the more comfortable this new way of approaching your professional experience will be.

Ready to go? Let's get started.

CHAPTER 2

Take Control

I have discovered in life that there are ways of getting almost anywhere you want to go, if you really want to go.

—Langston Hughes

Accept responsibility for every part of your current professional experience, and empower yourself to create a better one moving forward.

I once coached a woman who was smart, strong, driven, capable, well-spoken, poised, and knew exactly what she wanted—to direct a marketing team in a major organization. Yet she consistently found herself playing second fiddle to someone else, ending up in a manager position rather than the director-level position she truly desired. In one of our first conversations, I asked her why she didn't just start applying for every director-level position she could find, because geographic location wasn't a problem for her. She replied that she didn't think she would ever get them because she had never held a director-level position before, so why even try? She kept telling herself that success wasn't possible, and her actions (or lack thereof) followed this belief.

The problem is that the story she was replaying in her head over and over again had no basis in reality. Having been promoted from manager- to director-level positions myself, and having coached others through this process, I knew her stance was patently false—people make the leap in rank all the time. It was more a reflection of her own fear of rejection or failure than any competitive reality. But nothing I said or any evidence to the contrary could sway her. She was adamant that unless you've had a director-level position before, the competition was just too tough for her to be considered.

Then one day, she came across her dream job description for a senior director position at a great organization, and I immediately asked her when she was going to apply. She resisted at first, and then decided that if the application process didn't take more than fifteen minutes, she would give it a go . . . but if it took more than fifteen minutes, she wasn't going to bother. She did the bare minimum—submitting her LinkedIn profile for consideration without any personalized effort or cover letter—and called it a day.

I was incredulous, knowing that she had shot herself in the foot before even beginning the process. But to her it was a completely rational decision. She wasn't willing to spend more than fifteen minutes—less time than it takes to get ready in the morning, or run an errand, or catch up on the latest episode of your favorite TV show—to go after her "dream" job. Something that would have been life changing for her, and something that she had been coveting in the year that I had been communicating with her, was simply not deemed worthy of a little extra effort.

There was only one conclusion to make: She didn't really want it. There could be lots of reasons for that—perhaps she was afraid that if she got her "dream" job she would fail, or she was afraid of the rejection that might follow a job application. Regardless of what it was, she created a story that told her it was impossible to get the job so that she could abdicate her responsibility in the scenario. Her actions followed her belief in that story.

She would say she didn't have any choice at all in the situation— the realities of the professional world made attaining her dream job impossible. But creating that story in the first place was a choice. Ignoring contradictory evidence and experience was a choice. Not committing more than fifteen minutes to applying to what could have been her "dream" job was a choice. Could she have had a director-level job? Of course! With time and the right job-search strategy, it was absolutely possible. But she was the one who made the choice not to pursue it with unapologetic persistence, giving her potential employers no shot at really considering her for the position.

YOU CREATE YOUR PROFESSIONAL EXPERIENCE

Allow me to come right out and say it: If you are in a professional situation that you're not completely happy with, that's your fault. It's not your boss's fault, or your partner's fault, or your colleagues' fault. The buck stops with the person you look at in the mirror every day. You took the job you have and its responsibilities; accepted the pay; are at least half responsible for creating the relationships you've got with your coworkers, subordinates, and boss; and are responsible for the attitude you go in with each morning and the quality of the work you produce.

Everything you have right now—both the things that you love and the things that aren't so great—is a result of the choices that you have made. Those choices, most often, are a reflection of the story that you've created in your head regarding what is possible or what is most likely to make you happy. You are the only person who controls the stories you tell yourself.

SELF-MASTERY EXERCISE

Be mindful of the stories you're telling yourself. Take out your journal. Think about a time when you were feeling great about something going on at work—a project, a meeting, a colleague. Anything. Write down a few words that describe the story you were telling yourself at that time. It might look like one of these examples:

- I couldn't wait to start the project because I knew it was going to be successful.
- I was really looking forward to that meeting—I knew it was going to be a great moment for the team to collaborate and work together toward the goal.
- I couldn't wait for Johnny Jones to start—he has a great resume and I was so excited to have the chance to work with him.

Now let's look at the flip side. Think about a time when you were dreading something going on at work. Write down a few words that describe the story you were telling yourself then. Perhaps it looks like one of these:

- I hate my weekly meetings with my boss—they are always a waste of time.
- This client absolutely hates me.
- The people in that department are so inflexible.

We can always make the choice to look at things differently. Take another look at your negative story and ask yourself if there are different stories that you can tell yourself. Perhaps the example of weekly meetings with the boss becomes something like this: "My boss has her issues, but my weekly meeting with her is a chance for me to talk about the great work I've been doing. That's where I'll put my focus, no matter how she responds." Is that story any less true than the more negative version? No. It's simply forcing yourself to focus on the things that will enhance your happiness rather than detract from it.

Finally, think about what this exercise tells you about your ability to control your perspective. Next time you're having a bad day or a frustrating moment, simply change the story you're telling yourself and commit to the version that sets you up best for success.

YOU ALWAYS HAVE A CHOICE

There are few sentences I hate as much as "I have no choice."

"I have to stay in this job I hate—I have no choice."

"I have to bring work home with me instead of spending time with my family—I have no choice."

"I have to do what the boss says—I have no choice. He doesn't listen to me."

I was once interviewed for a radio program about happiness in the workplace, and the host wondered out loud if it was reasonable or fair for employees to expect to be happy at work. My response was immediate: Absolutely. It is 100 percent reasonable to expect to be happy in the place where you spend forty-plus hours a week in as long as you're doing your part to make it happen. The only time it becomes unreasonable is when you abdicate your responsibility in the process. That's like waking up one day and deciding to run a marathon without training for it—a monumentally bad idea that will probably leave you in a boatload of pain. Expecting your employer to do all the work for you in the happiness department is unreasonable because an employer cannot control your perspective or your behaviors—they simply provide the context you're operating in. Make no mistake, they aren't completely off the hook—they have their role to play as well (but that's a topic for a different book!). Your happiness at work starts with taking personal responsibility for the choices you make and the stories you tell yourself every single day.

That's the difference between people who are able to create their ideal work experience and those who never get there: The first group takes personal ownership over their career and understands that it's their actions that will make the difference, even if it's uncomfortable to pursue them. The latter does not. They blame everyone and everything around them for where they end up, because it's so much easier to blame someone else for the challenges you encounter than it is to look inward and take responsibility for where you are.

This is the piece that is hardest for most people because it involves a bit of a gut check. It's easy to look back at our lives and take credit for all the positive things that have happened. It's a lot harder to take a long look in the mirror and accept that you're also responsible for all of the not-so-good things. But you can't have one side of it be true without the other being true as well. You, and you alone, are responsible for your happiness, at work and in life. Every choice you make will impact your experience. You will get exactly what you should expect to get based on the stories you tell yourself and the actions you take.

All of this starts with embracing that you always have a choice. You make thousands of decisions every single day—what you think, what you do, and how you respond to every situation you find yourself in. When you say you don't have a choice, what you're really saying is that you don't like the potential outcomes of the options on the table, forgetting that abdicating responsibility for making a choice is a choice in itself. Doing so puts you in constant reactive mode—you're just responding to the things happening around you, waiting for other people to dictate the experience you have. It's as if you're riding in a kayak down a river without a paddle. Who knows . . . maybe it will be a smooth ride. But chances are you're going to encounter a waterfall at some point.

So why do people do it? Remember that in the previous chapter I told you that embracing the strategies in this book would push you outside of your comfort zone. And being uncomfortable is something that most of us avoid like the plague. Here's how:

- Opting out of negotiating for salary and benefits by just accepting what's offered to you.
- Refusing to make sacrifices like a pay cut or a new job that requires a move, even if that means getting closer to where you want to be professionally.
- Avoiding tough conversations with your boss or coworkers, even if they could lead to better relationships or resources you need to be successful.
- Saying yes to unnecessary projects or tasks, even if it means you'll need to work longer hours, throwing your work-life balance out of whack.

That's why so many people end up in unfulfilling work situations—they opt out of doing the things that would lead to a better situation because it might require doing things that are uncomfortable.

Now, a lot of people end up in reactive mode at some point in their career, so if it's happened to you, don't be too hard on yourself. Remember that we're not being judgmental here—we're simply observing. It's so easy to become reactive because very few of us are ever taught how to empower ourselves to be proactive during the natural course of our lives.

Consider why it might happen: All through primary and secondary education, you're told exactly what to do at all times. What to think, what to wear, what to read, what to learn for the test so you get into a good college, to stand in line and color inside the lines, etc. . . . You try to please everyone around you—your parents, teachers, friends, extended family—by playing by their rules. Sure, there are times when everyone tests boundaries and limits, but when you're still looking to Mom and Dad for the basic necessities, you probably don't push it too far.

We like to think this shifts for those who go to college after high school graduation, but it's just a little more freedom with a new set of boundaries. How many of us pick our school based on where our parents want us to go? How many more art, music, or philosophy majors would there be if people with a passion for those subjects weren't afraid of not getting a job after graduation? So, even though there is a greater sense of freedom, most college students are still operating within the bounds of what they think they need to do to be successful (or at least have Mom and Dad pay for school).

Whether you went to college or not, eventually you make it to

the real world. But most new grads aren't given a plethora of options for careers—they have to take the job that's offered. You
probably started with an entry-level job and weren't empowered to
do much of anything in your day-to-day. In that role, you were
likely an order-taker, doing what you were told while developing
expertise in whatever industry you work in. At this point in your
career, the promotions and raises were probably given to the people
who did the order-taking really well, so your professional success
depended on listening to what people needed and executing it
without much additional creative thought.

This could go on for years, because even when you work your
way up through the ranks, true empowerment and decision-making
is reserved for those at the very top. In most organizations, people
with "manager" or "director" titles don't really manage or direct
much of anything without the approval of their boss.

You may not have experienced every part of that story, but
chances are you experienced at least a portion of it. It's in fighting
the day-to-day battles—that continual grasp for empowerment
only to be slapped down over and over again—that causes people
to view their professional experience as something that largely
happens around them rather than something they are creating
for themselves.

Consider this moment a reset. It doesn't need to be this way, but
the only people who will find their way out of the vicious cycle are
the ones who make it a priority to take proactive control over their
experience. In buying a book like this, you've also made a choice—
the choice to regain control. It's never too late, and it's never impossible. But it does require undoing all the programming you've
had up to this point.

As we get into this, it will be easy to look back and kick yourself for not having done things differently. I'll keep reminding you to work through this book without judgment—it's not about beating yourself up for your choices. The past is gone, and you can't do anything to change it. Reliving it or relitigating things that have happened will not help you in any way and will only detract from your efforts to elicit different results in the future. There is not a person that has gone through life with a perfect track record of decision-making, and you won't be the first to hold that title. Instead, this is about moving forward mindfully, acknowledging how every step you choose to take will impact the future experiences you have.

YOU'RE RESPONSIBLE FOR YOURSELF

If we existed in bubbles by ourselves, the issue of choice wouldn't be a problem. It's when others are involved that it gets tricky. People have bad days, say things out of anger or stress, and can make it their mission to instill their own unhappiness in others. It's easy to give your power away when you either want to make someone happy, get their approval, or prevent them from being mad or disappointed. At work it's even more complicated because your boss or your colleagues may present ideas or projects in the form of a directive, leaving you feeling as though the decision has already been made for you and you have no choice but to follow along.

You are not responsible for what other people say or do. The only thing you're responsible for is how you react, both in terms of how you perceive the situation in your head (the story you tell yourself) and the actions you take as a result.

When we're faced with stressful situations, our first instinct is to go into fight-or-flight mode. This is a physiological response that is part of our survival instinct—our body releasing all sorts of hormones that do things like make your heart rate increase or your muscles tighten. This prepares our body to do one of two things: Either fight the element causing you stress or run away from it. Back when we were cave people, this response was mostly related to something coming to kill us. But we're not cave people anymore; today when we experience the fight-or-flight impulse, it's mostly a result of finding something emotionally stressful rather than being in any real physical danger.

For example, say you're in a meeting at work and a coworker starts to dress you down in front of half a dozen other people for a decision that wasn't your call. It's embarrassing and unfair—your colleague is trying to paint you as not being up to the task when you had nothing to do with it. When that happens, your fight-or-flight mode kicks in. If you're like most people, you'll instinctually do one of two things in this situation—either sit there quietly and not respond to avoid the conflict, or come at the person aggressively (perhaps more aggressively than necessary), asserting that it was not your call and there was nothing you could do about it. You may even start to view other people in the meeting as threatening as well, assuming they buy into what the person is saying and they're on his side. Then you're really off to the races because it's no longer just you against this one person—it's you against a half dozen other people. All your senses are heightened and it's very easy to overreact to the most minor perceived slight because your body is telling your subconscious that you are in danger, surrounded by people who want to do you harm.

Is that story objectively true? Of course not. Most of the people in the room probably thought that guy was just as much of a blowhard as you did. But our natural, evolutionary instinct is to react with a fight-or-flight response. The best way to combat this, and take back control when it starts to happen, is to become mindfully aware of when it's happening. You will be put in challenging situations at work. Being angry at the situation itself doesn't clear the easiest path to your best decision.

SELF-MASTERY EXERCISE

Take out your journal and consider the following questions: What does it feel like when you're under stress? Does your body shake? Feel tense? Does your heart race? Do you feel hot? Grind your teeth? Have a headache or a stomachache? Do you fidget? Do you start to experience impostor syndrome, hopelessness, anger, depression, or fear? Do you feel like you want to cry or lash out at the person causing you stress?

Now that you know what being under stress feels like for you from a detached perspective, you can use it. Next time you're in a situation at work that is causing you stress, take a moment to remind yourself of what is going on. You're not in any danger, and you have the power to create a different story about the situation from a beautifully detached perspective.

YOU'RE NOT A VICTIM

When challenging things happen at work, no matter their scale, it's easy to view yourself as the victim if you give into that fight-or-flight reaction. I love the way Mark Manson describes this in his book *The Subtle Art of Not Giving a F*ck*. He hits on the notion of fault versus responsibility, noting that we tend to overlap the two when we should be looking at them distinctly. Bad things happen to us. Challenging things happen. We can't control what other people say or do to us—it's not our fault. But it is our responsibility to control how we respond to it. Manson gives the example of someone leaving a baby on your doorstep—that's not your fault. Presumably you didn't leave a sign on your door that read "Abandoned Babies Welcome" and so you're not to blame for the fact that the bassinet found its way to your stoop. But you are responsible for what you do with that baby next, whether it's bringing him to a hospital or a fire station, or feeding him to the dog.

That's an extreme example. I'll make it more tangible to a professional experience. Several years ago, I was in a job at a large organization. It wasn't the best job I'd ever had—I worked on a challenging team that all felt like the unwanted stepchildren of the office and were constantly trying to prove their expertise worthy of consideration by the key decision-makers. I also wasn't the biggest fan of the leadership, who cultivated an environment that left the departments competing against one another for validation. But there were good things too—a solid mission that contributed value to society and a professional community in my industry that was filled with people I adored. Overall, it was your basic "meh" job. There were things I liked, things I didn't, and I wasn't really sure what I wanted to do with my career at the time, so I was more or less on cruise control.

Then one day, it all fell apart.

Or it seemed like it happened all in one day, but really it had been building for months. Unbeknownst to me, a subordinate viewed me as an obstacle to the next level of his career and had been waging a subtle campaign to endear himself to the right people to position himself for my job. It's important to understand that when people target us with malicious intent at work, all of it doesn't necessarily hit us immediately, and that's why it goes unnoticed. It's more like a slow boil. When you put a frog in a pot of boiling water, it will just jump right out and live to tell the tale. However, if you put the frog in a pot of water and bring it to a boil slowly, the frog won't even notice what's happening until it's too late.

Yes, in this instance I'm comparing myself to a frog. Bear with me.

Odd things, both at the office and in my professional community, would just happen here and there, but were so minor that I barely even gave them a moment of my attention. It took a lot of forms: A rumor, weird remark, or gossip I didn't understand the source of. People in my community that I considered friends unfriended me on Facebook (yes, it's a Millennial thing, but it's important!). My boss sent me emails specifically to admonish me for things I hadn't done. I was excluded from meetings. My ideas were taken and given to others to implement. Hindsight is twenty-twenty, but at the time it was hard to see a link between these occurrences when I was focusing my attention on my day-to-day tasks.

Then the pot started to boil: More extreme gossip and rumors, things that could no longer be called misunderstandings or miscommunications because they were just downright lies. People attacking me out of nowhere or sending me email tirades about what a horrible person I was. People in my professional community that I barely knew would look at me with daggers coming out of their eyes at networking events and wouldn't even shake my hand. None of it made sense to me, and it felt like I was on the receiving end of a mean girls attack in high school. I was in full-on fight-or-flight mode by this point. Sometimes I would come into work and try to fight the situation aggressively. Other times, I would just sit at my desk all day and not say a word to anyone.

And then one day, I lost my job. I was pulled into a room and fired by the highest-ranking man in the building without any warning that it was coming. Afterward, I called my boss—the person I actually reported to—and he didn't even know I was being dismissed. Weeks later, I found out from friends that the person I had recruited to the organization to work under me had gone around at industry events bragging that he'd endeared himself to the organization's leadership so that he could take my job and make more money. In the process of doing so, he'd destroyed my career, my reputation, and influenced people in my community to turn their backs on me without a hint of an explanation.

So, not a great place to be in. And I'm not going to tell you the story of someone who immediately got back on her feet and didn't let it bother her, because that did not happen right away. In the first week after I got fired, I cried. A lot. I felt more alone and discarded than at any other point in my life. My self-esteem plummeted. I didn't see any way out of it. After all, who would hire me now?

In the moment, it was very easy for me to paint myself the victim in the situation. After all, I couldn't have controlled what other people in the situation did or the campaign this person waged to take my job. Those things weren't my fault. But as Mark Manson would say, my responsibility was in how I responded. In retrospect, it's very easy to look back and say I made the choice to shut down, but in the moment I would have told you I had no choice.

A few weeks later, I made the choice to start getting back on my feet. I started applying for jobs, launched consulting services to fill the gap, and started doing fun things with my husband to keep me occupied in the meantime. And slowly, things started to get better. I found a new job at a company that was far better for me, and I started to integrate back into my professional community, even though there were people who still looked at me like I was the devil and, to this day, don't speak to me. I could have spent time worrying about what was said to them, and how to heal the relationship, but that would have just kept me in the past. That wasn't something I could control. Moving on was. And frankly, did I want to keep people in my life who would turn on me that easily? No. Instead, it gave me an opportunity to expand my relationships, and I made some great new friends. The experience also formed the basis for my doctoral dissertation on the subject of young professionals coping with being a target of workplace bullying and set me up to do the work I do today. It may have seemed like the end of my journey at the time, but it was just part of my path to where I am now. A very rocky part, perhaps. But a part nonetheless.

Being fired from a job when you were actively sabotaged by a colleague is about the worst thing that can happen to a professional. Almost any other experience you can have at work, apart from being sexually harassed or physically assaulted, pales in comparison to it. It disrupts your sense of self, because many of us consider our jobs to be a key part of our identity. If I had continued to see myself as a victim in the situation, I never would have been empowered to move on. Everything I needed was right in front of me—I just had to be in a place to reach out and grab it.

ACCEPT YOUR ROLE IN CREATING YOUR EXPERIENCE

I'll go one step further than Mark Manson does and say that not only do you need to acknowledge your responsibility to make choices in the face of a challenge; you've also got to accept the part you played in creating the challenge in the first place. Yes, you always play a role. You are responsible for everything you have, and that means accepting responsibility for the things that aren't so great.

Let's look at my example of being fired from that job. No, I was not responsible for that jackass's actions, but there is a lot I can take responsibility for. I wasn't really excited about the job, so I wasn't giving it 100 percent. I was annoyed by my coworkers always being cynical and didn't do a great job at communicating with them or building solid working relationships that would have made them question my subordinate's tall tales. Hell, I hired the guy in the first place, going out of my way to recruit him from another organization, telling myself the story that he was the only person who could fill that role effectively so that I didn't have to consider other candidates. All those things are my responsibility and are areas where I could have made better choices by changing the story I was telling myself. The goal wouldn't have been to keep my job, although that may have been an outcome (looking back, I'm thankful I lost it!). The goal would have been to create a better professional experience for myself for the time I was there.

Now let's take a less extreme example and look at the scenario of a coworker dressing you down in a meeting in front of a half dozen other people for something that wasn't your fault. Could you have checked in before the meeting to see if there was anything your coworker needed from you? Could you have done more to influence the decision that was made in the first place? During the meeting, was there a way you could you have communicated more effectively to steer the conversation from combative to collaborative? Could you have built a better relationship with that colleague so that he felt like you were on his team, eliminating the possibility that he would cut you down in front of others? No, you're not responsible for the dressing down . . . but you're not a helpless victim either.

Why is this step necessary? Because you're learning how to take control of your professional experience so that you can create an amazingly fulfilling one. You cannot be successful at that if you don't take responsibility by acknowledging the role you've played in creating the experience you currently have.

SELF-MASTERY EXERCISE

How are you creating your current professional experience? Take out your journal and make a list of the things you love about your current job and the things you hate. For each item on the list—the good and the bad—ruminate on your contribution to creating that part of your experience. The good stuff will be fun—it will allow you to create more good stuff moving forward. And for the not-so-good stuff, you'll get some ideas of how you could have done things differently to proactively avoid repeats of those same lessons in the future.

HOLD YOURSELF TO A NEW STANDARD

Work doesn't have to be a hard, arduous, or soul-sucking experience, but you will get out of it what you put into it. You make that decision. The standard I want you to hold yourself to from here on out is this: You—and you alone—are the creator of your professional experience. You will get exactly what you should expect based on the stories you tell yourself, which will dictate the actions you take, the goals you set, the relationships you build (or don't build), and the way you approach your work every single day. If you find yourself getting off track, pause and consider what you're contributing. Is it aligned with what you want to create? If not, how can you change it? This isn't going to eliminate all your challenges overnight, but it will lessen the knee-jerk reactions you have to them.

CHAPTER 3

Embrace Self-Mastery

Always be a first-rate version of yourself instead of a second-rate version of somebody else.

—Judy Garland

GOAL FOR THIS CHAPTER:

Get a sense of what your innate work style is and understand the unique strengths you bring to the office and where your blind spots are.

was running an errand one day at Trader Joe's, wearing a T-shirt that says "HR Tip #7: Not everyone is going to love you." It was a swag shirt that I got from an exhibitor at the Society for Human Resources Management annual conference, and I hadn't been wearing it for any particular reason—it just happened to be on the top of the pile. The man who rang up my purchases looked at it and commented, "Spoken like a true HR manager!" I shrugged and replied, "I'm an organizational psychologist—I'd be more likely to say 'others don't need to love you as long as you love yourself.'"

When I speak of self-mastery, that's what I mean: Learning to love yourself just the way you are—your strengths and all your glorious flaws. So often we look to other people to inform the way our experiences should be, lacking the understanding that what works for them might not be what works for us for any number of reasons. You already have all the tools you need to create an amazing work experience for yourself. This is about understanding what those tools are.

You make thousands of choices every single day, in and outside of work. Most of those choices are made on autopilot—they're things you do without thinking about them, because over the course of your life, they've become habit: What you eat for breakfast, the shampoo you use in the shower, the route you take to drive to work, what you put in your coffee, how you prep for meetings, the word choices you make when you send an email, how you react when a problem comes up, etc. When you break down the choices most people make day after day, there's a consistent pattern, because it's easier for us to keep doing the same thing we've always done. Mastering your work style will allow you to be constantly aware of why you're making the choices you are at work and understand the boundaries of your comfort zone. This will allow you to consciously push outside of that zone if that's what it takes to create the professional experience you want.

THERE IS NO RIGHT OR WRONG

You can tell a lot about people based on whether they are a cat person or a dog person—one is not inherently better or worse than the other, but they are very different. I'm a dog person, myself. My husband and I have two little dogs at home—a Chihuahua named Honey Robocop Poncho Tequila (she answers to both Honey and Robocop) and a Chiweenie (that's a Chihuahua Dachshund mix) named Kobe Taco Corona, Esq. As you might surmise from the fact that they have multiple names like royals, they are spoiled rotten and are completely ungrateful for how good they have it. And I'm one of *those* dog owners. If you follow me on Twitter, your feed will be blessed with pictures of my dogs doing everything under the sun—showing off their haircuts, having a beer bottle balanced on their heads, or just gazing longingly into the camera with those big eyes, a finely honed look that makes you want to reward them with all the bones in the world.

My point is this: I don't understand cat people.

Let's be honest—cats only really keep you around because you provide food and the occasional catnip or bowl of milk. It eludes me as to why someone would prefer them to the simple, pure, childlike love of a dog. I don't understand cat people in the way that I don't understand people who choose to never travel outside the town where they grew up, or choose to vacation somewhere cold and snowy instead of a warm, Caribbean beach, or choose to purchase a brown car when there are a whole bunch of other color options like red, blue, or black on the lot. In their head, these decisions make sense, but in mine, they simply do not compute.

But that doesn't mean I think cat people are bad people. It

doesn't mean I think they've made poor life choices. We're just built a little differently, and we value different things in our companions. But there's no right or wrong—different things make different people happy.

And this, in a nutshell, is what's going on with different work styles as well. Every single person comes to work with their unique makeup of preferences and tendencies that have been compiled over a lifetime of experiences. These are things like at what pace you like to work; whether you prefer collaboration or working on your own; if you cherish being in a leadership position or if you'd rather play a support role; whether you avoid conflict or whether it revs you up; if you like digging into data and analytics or if you just need a top sheet with the most critical information; and so on and so forth. These are all components that make up your unique work style.

As with cats and dogs, there's no work style that is right or wrong, good or bad. However, our coworkers don't come with cute fuzzy faces like dogs and cats, so it's easy to judge their quirks when we see something that's different from what we'd expect, or when someone does something in a way we don't appreciate. When you're judging others, you're really judging yourself—you're making a better/worse comparison between the way they do things and the way you do them. Remove the judgment and it suddenly becomes much easier to embrace what you (and they) bring to the table.

MASTER YOUR WORK STYLE

The first step toward mastering your work style is to understand what it is. You've probably taken a personality or a work-style test at some point in your life, whether it was something that was administered by your HR department or a quiz you took on Buzz-

Feed. So, you understand the idea—based on your answers to a few questions, you're able to understand what your default is, or the things you do when you're not actively thinking about it or dedicating extra energy to it.

When I'm assessing work style, I almost always use the DISC psychological model for a few reasons: It's been around for almost a century and has decades of rigorous examination behind it; it's easy for the average person to learn, understand, and utilize on a day-to-day basis; and in the thousands of DISC tests that I've administered, my clients find it to be freakishly accurate. Very rarely do I have a complaint (and when I do, it's usually about something the person doesn't want to admit about themselves). And finally, I like it because William Marston—the Harvard-educated psychologist who created the original DISC model—was also the creator of Wonder Woman. Talk about a supporter of personal empowerment!

There are a few things you need to know about work style before we dig into the specifics of what yours is.

Your work style is shaped by your life experiences

You formed your view of the world when you were very young—usually about seven years old—and those conceptions influence the stories you tell and the behaviors you choose for any given situation. By the time you reach adulthood, those tendencies are pretty well ingrained. It's not that you can't change a tendency—you can. It just takes some pretty dramatic life changes to initiate it and to allow those tendency changes to stick. With few exceptions, your work style will stay relatively consistent over the course of your career.

There are a few things that don't impact your work style that
may surprise you:

- Intelligence. Smart people come in all shapes and sizes! There's
  no known correlation between a person's aptitude and their
  work style, though pursuing ongoing education may shift your
  style because of the experience and knowledge gained in that
  process.
- Gender. Some of the work styles we'll look at will seem more
  stereotypically masculine, and others will seem more feminine,
  but the difference between how many men and women test into
  those styles is not statistically significant. Women are just as
  likely to have more "masculine" work styles as men are, and
  vice versa.
- Generation. Log on to any business-related website and you'll
  see an article about generational differences in the workplace.
  Generations may make it easy to categorize people, but statistically there is no difference in the styles they bring to the
  office—their distribution is even among the styles we'll look at.

Your work style does not tell you what you can and can't do

It's very easy for some people to use work-style assessments as a
crutch, insisting that the test tells them they are incapable of doing
certain things. Au contraire. Your work style tells you where your
comfort zone is, but you can always push past the boundaries of
your comfort zone. It just requires more focus and energy to do so
than it does to remain safely inside of it. It is absolutely critical to
understand that creating an amazing professional experience for
yourself will often require you to push outside of your comfort

zone. The only thing that holds you back from doing so is a willingness to do so.

We're going to look at four distinct work styles, and you'll be more likely to pull your tendencies from one or two of them than the others. But from a psychological perspective, every single person is a blend of all four styles—your results just tell you what you're more inclined to do when you're not thinking about it. It's like the clothes in your closet. You probably have all sorts of colors of shirts. Black, blue, green, red . . . they're all there in your closet, waiting for you to wear them. But you think you look nicer (and therefore feel more comfortable) in some colors than others, so you tend to wear those more. Your work style functions in the same way. You can do anything anyone else can do—those talents are already there, just waiting for you to use them. It just might take you a bit more energy because it's not the thing you're used to doing.

Another way to look at this might be the introvert-extrovert scale. If a person would rather curl up at home with a good book than go out to a party on a Friday night, they are probably an introvert, meaning they gain their energy from being alone. An extrovert would do the opposite, gaining their energy from being around other people. But can an introvert go to a party on a Friday night and have a good time? Yes! Can an extrovert enjoy an evening of staying home and vegging on Netflix? Of course! Your work style doesn't tell you what you can and cannot do—you're a multidimensional human being with free will, after all. It simply tells you what you're most likely to do when you're not putting extra effort in.

Learning this information will help you become more comfortable doing things that are uncomfortable, because you'll be able to put them in context. We shy away from things that cause us pain, in both the physical sense and the emotional sense. For some people, going to a networking event or getting up in front of a group to give a presentation is a very painful experience! Think about those times when you get nervous at work—you have a very real physical reaction to it, just like you do when you have a nightmare. Your heart starts to race, your whole body tenses up, your hands shake, you may even start to sweat. You may not have gotten punched in the arm, but your body is telling you that you are in pain, and that emotional pain is just as real as something that causes a bruise.

When that happens, recognize it's happening because you're moving outside of your comfort zone. If you're aware of it, you can remind yourself of the reason you're pushing yourself—because it serves your goals. Understanding that will help you push through the discomfort, making the next time you do it a little bit easier.

Beware the freebie DISC profile

Walk down a toilet paper aisle in the supermarket and you'll have dozens of options to choose from. And toilet paper can be so expensive! Why not make it easy and just go with the cheapest? How different could it be from the other options?

Of course, that's a ridiculous question—anyone who has ever experienced the cheapest roll of toilet paper knows exactly why you spend the extra money. Your return on investment is clear in the extra comfort that higher quality (and softer!) toilet paper provides.

But put something like a psychological assessment in front of people and they are instantly chintzy with themselves. They want the cheapest option available, and that usually means free. This chapter will walk you through an exercise to get a general sense of what your work style is, but it does not include a full assessment that will give you really specific information. I would if I could, but I also don't want the book to cost seventy-five dollars!

Since you're not getting a full DISC assessment here, it might be tempting to read this chapter and want to search for those free options. Trust me, you'll find them! DISC is a psychological model, not a brand of test—that means that anyone, anywhere can use it to develop their own free assessments. However, there are no checks on those companies to make sure their assessments actually work or provide you with the accurate, meaningful results you're looking for.

So a word of caution: Beware the free assessment. I have this conversation with people all the time:

Them: "I took a DISC test but it didn't sound like me at all."

Me: "Was it a free online one?"

Them: "Yes."

Me: "Those aren't accurate. The ones you pay a little bit for have teams of people that are constantly researching, refining, and improving the tests and will give you results that are more on point."

This is a perfect example of getting what you pay for. On my website (www.zenyourwork.com), I offer the highest quality assessment that I've been able to find as an option and will personally vouch for it as being accurate, reliable, and valid. But truth be told, if you decide to take a full assessment, I don't particularly care if you get it from me or from someone else—I care that you have a resource to help you advance your career. This is a tool you can use for decades in any type of professional situation. Can you go for the cheapest option? Yes. But like toilet paper, it's simply not a good idea and you'll probably regret it later.

DISCOVER YOUR WORK STYLE

You've made it through the preliminary information, and now it's time to dig in and discover your work style. DISC looks at how likely you are to show attributes from four different types: Dominant (D), Influencer (I), Steady (S), and Conscientious (C). Most people gravitate to one or a combination of two of these four styles.

Your pace of work

To figure out where you are, you'll consider your placement on two different axes. On the first, consider the pace at which you like to work. Would you be more likely to describe yourself as fast-paced, assertive, bold, and dynamic, or would you be more likely to say that you're more moderately paced, methodical, careful, and thoughtful? Use the chart on the next page, or draw it in your journal, and put a marker where you see yourself on this scale.

Here's a hint: Most people aren't in the 50/50 range on either of the scales we'll look at—we tend to veer more toward one or the other. Remember, there is no right or wrong answer here. It can be easy to think that the grass is always greener on the other side, and to glamorize tendencies you see in other people that you wish were easier for you, but every work style has both strengths and challenges. The more honest you are about your tendencies, the more accurate your results will be from this quick assessment. If you're

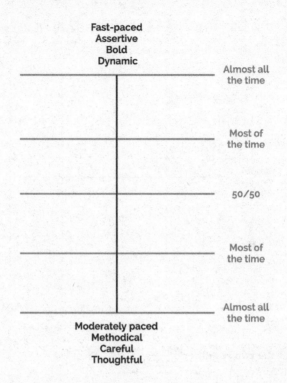

having a tough time with this, ask someone you trust—a friend, co-worker, or partner—what they would say about you. Sometimes we just need someone a little more objective to tell us where we stand.

How you receive information

Next, we're going to look at how you receive information. When you're at work, would you say you're more likely to look at things with a questioning, logical, objective, and sometimes skeptical point of view, or are you more likely to be accepting and receptive of information and present a warm, agreeable demeanor? Put a marker where you fall on this scale.

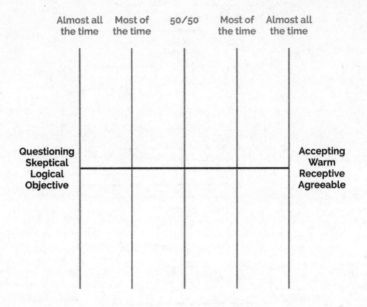

Put the two together!

Finally, you put the two together! Wherever your marker fell on the vertical and horizontal axes in the above two scales, combine them and find where you are on the DISC model.

- If you're more likely to be fast-paced and questioning, you have a Dominant work style.
- If you're more likely to be fast-paced and accepting, you have an Influencer work style.
- If you're more likely to be moderately paced and accepting, you have a Steady work style.
- And if you're more likely to be moderately paced and questioning, you have a Conscientious work style.

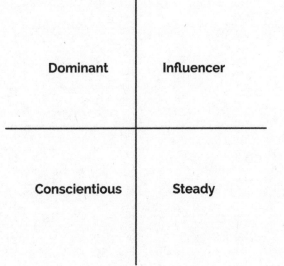

You may have a primary and a secondary style

Remember, you are a blend of all four work styles, so you will likely be a little bit of each. However, rather than just being a straight D, I, S, or C, most people tend to default to two styles. For example, you may be a combination of the D and the I styles, or the S and the C styles, meaning your comfort zone lies between the two and you'll have tendencies from both.

Take another look at where your marker is on the above graph. If you placed it in the relative middle part of your primary style's square, you will typically default more toward that style. However, if your marker is closer to one of the other styles, that tells you what your secondary style is. For example, if you have D as your primary style, but your marker in the above graph is really close to the I line, then I is your secondary style.

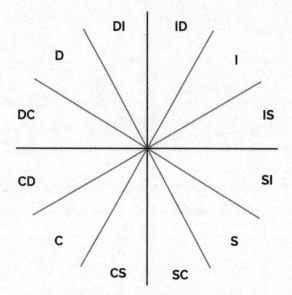

Use the graph above as a guide. Try transposing your marker from the graph on the previous page and put it in the exact same spot on the graph above, with the combination styles more delineated. That will tell you if you tend to veer toward one or two different styles. If you have two styles, the dominant of the two will be indicated by the first letter.

Note that there are styles that mix well and others that tend not to. For example, very few people will have tendencies from both the C and the I style, or the D and the S style, because those tendencies are direct opposites on almost all accounts. That's not to say that it doesn't happen—I have seen it in a handful of cases. If you find yourself straddling two divergent styles, choose the one that you feel most strongly about for our purposes here.

WHAT IT ALL MEANS

Now you know what your work style is! Let's look at each type so that you can discover what you're great at and what you need to watch out for. You'll use this information to guide the rest of your work with this book, reading each chapter with the understanding of the choices you are most likely to make, and how they may or may not serve you in any given situation.

You'll want to read the information in this chapter in two different ways:

- First, read about the one or two styles that you gravitate to. Use your journal to make notes about the things you agree with and those you don't.
- Next, read about the styles that are different from you. Consider the different approaches they take to solve problems, present information, and relate to others. Consider how you might try those things in your day-to-day. The better you become at adapting to techniques that are outside of your comfort zone, the more successful you'll be, because you'll have a bigger arsenal of skills to choose from.

The Dominant Style

Those with the Dominant (D) work style are most likely to be considered "natural leaders." They're assertive, bold, direct, results-oriented, forceful, firm, strong-willed, challenging, and skeptical. Although most D's are not true narcissists, those with narcissistic personalities would likely fall into this style.

People with this work style tend to like a faster pace, because it allows them to build momentum and get quick results. Because they want to get things out the door quickly, they have a tendency to step over established processes or rules that might hold them back. This inclination to question the way things have always been done can be a strength. After all, some rules are made to be broken! But sometimes, taking a minute or two to understand why the rule is there can help a D out. The rule may have been put into place to address a problem, and may help a D avoid making the same mistake twice.

People with the D style like to be in charge. They exude the confidence that can help others feel great about bold (sometimes intimidating!) ideas. This is particularly true if the D is on a project with a group that doesn't have clear leadership—it's natural for them to try to step into that role to provide the team with direction and inspiration. If you have this style, make sure you're flexing your leadership muscle in a way that brings other people along with you. You'll likely be on teams with people who are more reserved and soft-spoken, but they have strengths where you have weaknesses and will still bring good ideas to the table. Make sure you give them a chance, instead of dismissing their ideas out of hand in order to move on quickly. They're probably much better at identifying problems than you are, and if you listen to what they have to say, you set yourself up to get the win you're looking for.

D's have one of the more skeptical styles, and don't put a lot of emphasis on the warm and fuzzy emotional stuff. They have no patience for small talk and tend to view optimism and kind words from colleagues with suspicion, assuming they're saying it because they want something. They also have a competitive streak—the idea of losing or failing to achieve results is much scarier to them than it is to other work styles. This tendency to achieve can come across to others as very direct and intense. The key to a D's success is to balance their drive and ambition with taking advantage of the help and different perspectives other work styles offer.

At the end of the day, people with the D style are the ones who make things happen. They take bold action and are willing to challenge assumptions. Organizations need leaders who inspire those around them to achieve more than they thought possible, and this style brings that in spades.

If you're a D, here are some things to keep in mind as you work your way through the rest of the chapters in this book. Refer back to this list as you get to each chapter and read it with that context in mind.

- **Always be aware:** You move very quickly, almost as if you are constantly being guided by instinct. In the process, you may have a tendency to overlook the full nuance and context that you find yourself in. Slowing down just a bit will allow you to detach and take a full look around you to cover your bases.
- **Set your own goals:** You can keep your eye on the prize like no other and will have no problem putting your stake in the ground. Take care that the goals you set are achievable—you have a tendency to think you can do more than is realistic. But sometimes that lack of realism is also good—it pushes you to amazing heights.
- **Become unapologetically optimistic:** You have a naturally skeptical disposition, making unapologetic optimism way outside of your comfort zone. It's going to feel fake and inauthentic to

you. That's okay—the more you do it, the easier it will become. Just remind yourself that this isn't about being warm and fuzzy—it's about meeting your goals.

- **Build amazing relationships:** Relationships at work are tricky for you, because people are either going to love working with you or be intimidated and/or annoyed by you. Take care to get to know the people you're working with and adapt your style to the person in front of you as much as you can.

- **Find your beginner's mind:** You're very quick to form judgments about almost any situation you're in. Integrating meditation into your day will help you learn to quiet your mind so you can take things at face value.

- **Boost your confidence:** You're going to have no problem with expressing confidence. In fact, other work styles should emulate your approach! But take care that the people you're in front of don't view it as arrogance. Use questions to engage your colleagues in conversation, and genuinely listen to their answers. Don't just wait for your turn to talk. Remember, it's not the "you" show—you're part of a team. The more you help others win, the more you win yourself.

- **Working with enemies:** D's can be the classic bull in the china shop. They want things done their way and will leave a trail of bodies in their wake. Never underestimate the importance of bringing people along.

- **Discover career clarity:** You won't have much trouble rising through the ranks if you want to—D's have the natural executive profile. However, make sure that it's what you want. Having the highest ranking job in the company may give you money, it may give you prestige . . . but it won't necessarily make you happy.

- **Find your balance:** You have a stronger inclination than most to be a workaholic, because the hustle of getting things done is really exciting to you. Make sure you're taking the time to get your work-life balance in check. It isn't a nice-to-have. It's a nonnegotiable.

The Influencer Style

Those with the Influencer (I) style are the most fun to be around at work. They're active, dynamic, outgoing, high-spirited, lively, enthusiastic, optimistic, and empathizing. The best way to describe an I is that they are the "people person" of the office. They're connectors. They have an extensive network of friends and colleagues, and a natural charisma and unapologetic optimism that draws people in and gets them really excited about their ideas and goals.

I's greatest strength lies in their ability to communicate, whether one-on-one or in small or large groups. They use everything they have to express their ideas, from the excitement in their voice to their body language, complete with big hand gestures. This is great for getting people fired up, but I's should be aware that for work styles with a more skeptical disposition, that enthusiasm can be a turnoff. Make sure you've got a good handle on the work styles of the people you're presenting to because a one-size-fits-all approach does not apply. Use the same exercise you used to figure out your own style to identify the styles of the people you're presenting to and adapt accordingly.

People with the I style will be happiest working in groups, whether they're formally collaborating or just shooting the breeze after a meeting. They can use their gifts in brainstorming sessions to get people excited about the big ideas and possibilities.

Storytelling is their best friend—they can use it to make their ideas tangible and show how they can be applied in the real world.

One of the biggest challenges that the influencer style faces is, for lack of a better term, a massive case of ADD. They tend to move quickly and love to have a bunch of projects going on at the same time. Though this tactic might not work well for those with other work styles, it's great for the I's in the group as long as they also find the discipline to commit to deadlines and focus on follow-through. Sometimes they overestimate their ability to get things done, leaving them in a constant game of catch-up that just stresses them out.

Their positive outlook is one of the greatest assets for our influencers because looking on the bright side will almost always make them more successful in their careers. However, this positivity can become problematic when they avoid unpleasant but necessary conversations like the plague. For I's, all work is personal and they never want to be the bearer of bad news. That means that sometimes they hold on to negative things until they reach a breaking point. If you're in the I style, make sure you're managing your stress and looking for ways to express your emotions and frustrations. No one will think less of you and this expression will get you back on track with your optimistic outlook again.

If you're an I, here are some things to keep in mind as you work your way through the rest of the chapters in this book. Refer back to this list as you get to each chapter and read it with that context in mind.

- **Always be aware:** You always try to see the best in people, and it's very easy for you to give a person or situation the benefit of the doubt. And that's wonderful, but sometime a dash of skepticism would do you good. Not too much, just enough to remember that not everyone has the good-natured approach you do.

- **Set your own goals:** Though you understand conceptually that it may be necessary, goal setting and tracking your progress will feel like a chore to you—it doesn't seem fun. So find a way to make it fun. Use a planner with lots of colors and treat the process like a game, even giving yourself a little reward at the end of the week if you hit your targets.

- **Become unapologetically optimistic:** Of all the work styles, you will have zero problem with unapologetic optimism. In fact, you'll be the role model for others in this regard. Take that role seriously—they need to see you expressing optimism. When you do it, you're serving the team.

- **Build amazing relationships:** You're a natural relationship builder and someone your coworkers genuinely enjoy working with. But keep in mind that you need to tone down the enthusiasm with some of your more skeptical colleagues or they will be suspicious of your motives!

- **Find your beginner's mind:** You can get really excited about new ideas, but if you've had a bad experience or outcome with a project or task in the past, it may leave a sour taste in your mouth. Remember, what's happened in the past doesn't matter. Try to free it from your mind as much as possible and focus on the work you have in front of you right now.

- **Boost your confidence:** You have no problem getting yourself in front of people, but where you might struggle is in having a clear, concise message. Make sure you prep your talking points—and stick to them! That will help people follow along with what you're saying.

- **Working with enemies:** Though relationships are certainly your game, you detest working with people if you think they don't like you. Depersonalize the situation by reminding yourself that it's not you, it's them.

- **Discover career clarity:** Make sure you're in a profession and a role that enhances your experience. Generally speaking, I's do not excel in highly detail-oriented roles, like accounting or IT. It's not to say you can't, but those professions don't take advantage of your natural gifts. You need to be in a role that has a social component to be really happy—you feed off the energy of others and enjoy collaboration.

- **Find your balance:** Everyone likes to have fun, but if you're an I, you need it in your life. Whatever fun looks like to you, make sure you have time every week to do those things—to get out and be social with your friends, do things with your family, or go out and meet new people. The strength of your out-of-work life will translate to your satisfaction in the office.

The Steady Style

Everyone loves working with those with the Steady (S) style because they're agreeable, receptive, accommodating, patient, even-tempered, tactful, humble, calm, and thoughtful. They just make things easy. They rarely lead the team, but they make exceptionally strong members of it because they place the good of the group as their top priority, even over individual achievement. Unlike the more competitive work styles, people with the S style will be the first to share credit for victories with others, which can be both good and bad. Yes, it's great to share the wealth, but it's also okay to save some accolades and kudos for yourself.

Those with the S style have a strong need for harmony above all else and find it difficult to push back or say no even if they are being inconvenienced. They want others to be happy and will never be the first to rock the boat. Their challenge is to find a balance between supporting others and taking care of their own needs—if they don't, they'll watch others get promoted ahead of them while their career stagnates.

Unlike the Dominant or the Influencer styles, S's tend to like a more cautious pace and may experience anxiety when those around them want to step on the gas. Some think S's are afraid of change, but that's not true—they want to make sure things have been thoroughly thought through to avoid any problems or unpleasantries. Sometimes they take this a little too far, focusing too much on what could go wrong with the project rather than the potential benefits of it. Remember, sometimes it's okay to move forward with something when you're 70 percent sure of the result, rather than holding off and waiting for a 100 percent that might never come.

People with this work style tend to be more soft-spoken than others and may keep their ideas to themselves. When they do speak up, they might appear wishy-washy—a stark contrast to the brazen confidence of the Dominant style. This happens because they qualify their statements or offer alternatives without being asked to do so. The intention is good, but some people read it as indecisive. If you're an S, make sure you're presenting your ideas confidently, in a way that will make others more likely to get on board.

No work environment would be complete without those in the S style—their dependability and support of others is critical to a cohesive team. They are admired for their humble and tactful manner, but this is their greatest challenge as well. It leads to them underestimating their contribution to the organization. If you're an S, understand that those on your team would feel lost without you. Embrace it. Love it. And then use it to contribute to the team's success and advance your own career at the same time.

If you're an S, here are some things to keep in mind as you work your way through the rest of the chapters in this book. Refer back to this list as you get to each chapter and read it with that context in mind.

- **Always be aware:** You don't have any trouble with awareness when it comes to other people, but you probably don't leave much left over for yourself. Always remember that your first responsibility is to take care of your own needs—when you do that, you put yourself in a better position to support the team.
- **Set your own goals:** You're so focused on others that you might let their needs overtake your own priorities, both professionally and personally. It's okay to put your stake in the ground and say, "This is what I want." Allow yourself that.
- **Become unapologetically optimistic:** You don't have the enthusiasm of the Influencer style but generally you can look on the bright side. The exception is when you are thinking about embarking on new projects—it's harder for you to express optimism because you may be worried about how it might impact things already in place in the organization. Ask yourself, "What am I afraid of?" as a way to pinpoint the problem causing the anxiety, and then look for a way around it.
- **Build amazing relationships:** People love working with you because you take care of them and are perfectly happy to put their needs before your own. Make sure you balance this by clearly

communicating your needs. S's can internalize a lot of grief from other people until it builds up and one day they explode (which is a scary thing for others to see because they're usually so steady!). Relationships are a two-way street—you may go overboard and give, give, give without taking anything for yourself in return.

- **Find your beginner's mind:** You're very quick to form judgments about almost any situation you're in. Integrating meditation into your day will help you learn to quiet your mind so that you can look at things for their face value.
- **Boost your confidence:** You're more known for your quiet demeanor than your confidence. It's not that you don't have good ideas that are worth listening to—it's how you present them, offering diplomatic solutions with options to please everyone. Learn to speak with assertiveness and to quiet that little voice in the back of your head that says you might be wrong.
- **Working with enemies:** Your style will excel in this area. Your challenge will be not internalizing other people's negative thoughts, demeanors, and perspectives. They're miserable in their own special way, but it has nothing to do with you. That's their problem to sort out. Don't make it yours.
- **Discover career clarity:** Challenge yourself to go bigger than you feel comfortable with. Dream about what you would do if you put your needs before anyone else's. Remember, you're not making a permanent commitment—it's just a thought experiment. You don't have to go after it until you're ready.
- **Find your balance:** Balance is about putting your needs first. When you do that, you put yourself in a much stronger position

to support other people. Challenge yourself to make sure you're doing things that are just for you—not just for your family or friends or partner.

The Conscientious Style

The Conscientious (C) style is the most logical of them all! C's are careful, methodical, reserved, private, systematic, precise, analytical, and objective. There is no work style that loves their processes and procedures as much as a C—they relish developing and adhering to systems that maintain quality. However, sometimes that desire to maintain strict control over their processes can get them in trouble, inhibiting their ability to work well with people of other styles.

Those with the C style tend to want to keep to themselves at work. If they had it their way, they'd probably work in an office with a closed door and the shade drawn to ward off interruptions. It's not that they're being antisocial—it's that this solitude allows them to get really absorbed in what they're doing and to focus on all the details. However, others can take it the wrong way. The hardest lesson for a C to learn is that it's relationships at work that make people successful.

Though they keep to themselves quite a bit, it's very easy for C's to become angry or annoyed when they feel like their processes are being ignored. And that annoyance can quickly lead to interpersonal conflict. In fact, rarely do I come across a strong interpersonal conflict in organizations that doesn't involve at least one person with a lot of C in them. When someone rubs them the wrong way, they hold on to it and can wreak havoc on team morale if they don't learn to temper this inclination. It can help if they remind themselves that there is always more than one way to solve a problem or meet a particular goal, even if it makes them uncomfortable to put someone else in the driver's seat.

The most valuable contribution that C's make to the organization is their attention to detail. They live and breathe in spreadsheets, know how all the parts work together, and have the ability to analyze complex situations and data sets in a precise manner—they find all the opportunities that people in other styles have trouble uncovering. Their greatest challenge is to do this in a way that lifts up and supports the team. The sooner they find the value in playing well with others, the more successful they will be!

If you're a C, here are some things to keep in mind as you work your way through the rest of the chapters in this book. Refer back to this list as you get to each chapter and read it with that context in mind.

- **Always be aware:** Your focus on logic and reason can make it difficult to see things from other people's points of view, but the world is not black-and-white. Embrace your logical mind for this—if you make someone else feel like you don't value them, what can you expect to get from them in return?
- **Set your own goals:** Committing to goals will be one of your strongest attributes—you'll have no problem breaking down the big picture into small moving parts. Just don't allow yourself to get stuck too much in the weeds. Zoom out every once in a while to make sure you're still going in the right direction.
- **Become unapologetically optimistic:** If there's a style that can pinpoint everything that could go wrong in every possible situation, it's you. It's not that you're being intentionally negative, but you can come across as unnecessarily combative. Only

5 percent of the population is motivated by critical feedback—think about what that means when you're the person in the room who's always pointing out the problems.

- **Build amazing relationships:** To put it bluntly, people with the C style aggravate the heck out of their coworkers. Part of it is that they're intimidated by your intelligence, but the other part is that they perceive you as just plain inflexible. You think you're winning when you get people to do things a certain way, but you're really losing because you don't make them feel great about doing it. Try telling yourself the following story: "When I'm making others feel good, I'm helping myself and meeting my goals."

- **Find your beginner's mind:** Staying in the present is going to be challenging. For you, it's very logical—things that have happened in the past should inform what you're doing now. The problem is that you don't let go of them and move on—you keep them in your back pocket for months or years at a time, just waiting for the right moment to whip them out. Meditation will help you, if you can push outside your comfort zone and give it a try.

- **Boost your confidence:** Confidence is not something you are lacking—you believe there's a right and a wrong, and the right way is your way. What will hold you back is debating, or even arguing, with people who disagree with you—it takes the focus off what you want and puts it on the fight. Remember that not everyone enjoys conflict. Instead of debate, ask questions and engage in a dialogue.

- **Working with enemies:** When you have an office enemy, it's probably because they're just as strong-willed and stubborn as you are, and you're butting heads. Try to focus on what you have in common instead of where you disagree.

- **Discover career clarity:** Be hyper aware of what you like doing in a job and what you don't. That includes managing a team. A lot of C's are not happy in management positions and are much better suited to being individual contributors.
- **Find your balance:** There's more to life than work. Allow yourself to let go and have fun. Don't take your computer home. Spend time on hobbies you really enjoy. This will give your brain time to decompress so you can get back to focusing on all those details on Monday morning.

REVIEW WHEN YOU NEED TO

As you work through the chapters in this book, you may want to come back and reference this chapter, as well as any notes you took in your journal, to remind yourself of what it says about your innate work style and the challenges you might face as you address the concepts in each subsequent chapter. This is particularly true if you're finding resistance to an idea—look at the notes on your work style here and try to suss out why that resistance exists. If it's something that's outside your comfort zone, try to get yourself to push through and give it a try. Becoming comfortable with being uncomfortable is the only path to growth. Embrace it!

PART II

own your perspective

When I was in school studying public relations, there was one concept they drilled into us over and over again: When it comes to publicity and press coverage, perception is reality.

It turns out that concept is also true when it comes to being able to zen your work . . . except that in this context the most important perception you need to worry about isn't that of the people you work with. It's the perception you bring with you to the office every day. If you're inclined to see the worst possible attributes in every person or situation you encounter, you will! But that doesn't mean it's what will serve your goals or help you create an amazing work experience for yourself.

In this section, you'll become aware of the different tricks your brain plays on you that get in the way of maintaining a positive perspective; develop a new strategy for achieving personal goals; and learn what it means to be unapologetically optimistic.

CHAPTER 4

Always Be Aware

The more clearly you understand yourself and your emotions, the more you become a lover of what is.

—Baruch Spinoza

GOAL FOR THIS CHAPTER:

Approach your day-to-day from a beautifully detached perspective and learn the tricks your brain plays on you to throw you off course.

Meb Keflezighi was thirty-nine years old when he won the 2014 Boston Marathon. He had been a world-class marathoner for years, winning a silver medal for the United States in the Olympic marathon ten years prior in 2004. But the 2014 Boston Marathon was special. Every long-distance runner dreams of running in the Boston Marathon, and Meb wanted to be in Boston on that day, one year after the 2013 bombings, to reclaim

the race. Of the 36,000 people who started the race, there were
only a very few who had a shot of winning. The best in the world
came out to compete, including the number one and number two
ranked men's marathoners in the world. Meb wasn't even ranked in
the top ten. No one thought he had any chance of winning. So
when he turned onto Boylston Street in the lead with just a third of
a mile left to go, the TV commentators were so shocked that one
of them said he was going to need oxygen because he wasn't going
to make it through the broadcast from sheer excitement. All three
of them screamed "Unbelievable!" as he crossed the finish line.
Pushing forty years old, Meb became the first American to win the
greatest road race in the world in over thirty years, a feat that had
been deemed thoroughly impossible.

So how did he do it? I think if you asked him, he would agree
that the emotional connection he had to the event—to bring a win
home for the United States on that very special day—drove him
beyond what everyone thought was possible. There are a lot of
times when our passion and that intangible emotional drive are our
best friends, giving us a distinct competitive advantage over others
who may not have as strong of a connection to the end result.

Sometimes that's true in the office. Passion and drive in your
professional experience can be wonderful and push you beyond obstacles so you can achieve your goals. But if you really think about
having that passion in your career, it's probably the exception
rather than the rule. In the day-to-day, creating a fulfilling experience is much more like a game of chess than it is an athletic event.
This distinction is what causes confusion for many people—they
may have the right intention, but they are playing by the rules of
the wrong game.

In a marathon, the adrenaline you have running through your

body helps you cross the finish line because it's a game of physical endurance. Chess is a head game. You have to zoom out and look at the whole board, knowing how each piece moves and thinking three steps ahead of your opponent. When you get emotionally involved in a game of chess, it doesn't enhance your decision-making; it diminishes it. Watch the masters play and you'll see they are as cool as cucumbers, thoughtfully pondering every possible move, seeing how it impacts the whole board and the moves they could make in the future, and considering the moves their opponent might make in response.

I'll say this another way: They are aware. They've found their zen and are working from a beautifully detached, nonjudgmental place, conscious of what their actions mean within the context of the environment they're working in. When their opponent takes one of their pieces, they don't get upset. They look at the board and ask themselves what they're going to do about it to get closer to checkmate. In fact, sometimes they may sacrifice one of their pieces, knowing that a small loss may lead them to a bigger win.

One of the key skills you've got to master to find your zen at work is to reserve judgment. That will allow you to be hyperaware of the context you're working in and the stories you're crafting in your head, so (when necessary) you can change those stories for ones that get you toward your goals. Our brain doesn't always make this easy for us, and understanding why it doesn't will help you put it in perspective.

THE TRICKS OUR BRAINS PLAY

A few years back, I was traveling from my home in New Hampshire to Austin, Texas, to go to a conference, and I found myself at the airport at eight a.m. on a Sunday morning with nothing to read except an advanced quantitative research textbook I had thrown in my bag on the way out the door. As fascinating as that subject is, it isn't the type of light reading one might enjoy on a Sunday morning, so I stopped by the airport bookstore and picked up a paperback bestseller.

I got on the plane and sat down next to a nice-looking older gentleman in an expensive tailored suit. He was on the phone laughing and joking with his wife, and I quietly opened my book and started reading. He had to hang up when they shut the cabin door a few minutes later, and he turned to me and struck up a conversation. Inevitably, he asked me what I was reading. Now, I don't embarrass easily . . . but I may have turned a bit red when I showed him my copy of *Fifty Shades of Grey* and confessed that I was reading smut. Luckily for me, he laughed, pulled out a copy of his *Wall Street Journal* and proceeded to point out three different stories about men in high-level corporate and government positions getting caught having affairs and having to resign because of it. Then he said, "Look! I'm reading smut too!"

What does any of this have to do with creating your ideal work experience? Absolutely nothing. But now I know I have your attention because that's how your brain is hardwired to work. It's already played a little trick on you in the last two paragraphs.

A really simple way to understand this is to think of the brain as split into three different parts: The old brain, midbrain, and new brain. The old brain was the very first part of our brain to develop, way back when we were cavemen, and it is interested in three things: Survival, food, and sex. It's constantly scanning our environment looking for those three things, and when it finds one of them, it perks up like a dog that has just seen a bone, telling you this is something important—pay attention to it. That's how I know I have your attention—mentioning something culturally related to sex might not be HR approved, but it does do the trick. (I could have also threatened your life or food source, but this way was a little nicer.)

Your brain does this subconsciously—you're not aware of the fact that you're constantly looking for those three things. Your brain takes in and sifts through a ton of information that doesn't ever reach your conscious awareness—eleven million pieces of information every single second across your five senses. Of those eleven million pieces, we are aware of about forty of them. So there's a huge disconnect between the amount of information your brain takes in and what you're actually conscious of.

You've seen this in action more than you might imagine. For instance, think of a time when you've driven home from work at night. You get in your car at the office parking lot, start driving down the road, make it all the way home, pull into your driveway . . . and then you realize that you don't remember driving home. It's not that you fell asleep—you were just on autopilot because nothing eventful happened on the drive. But if a deer had run out in front of your car, or if another car had suddenly slammed on its brakes in front of you, your old brain would have sprung into action and told you to pay attention so you could react and avoid getting hurt.

Your old brain is your primary decision-maker, filtering your choices through the lens of "food, survival, sex." However, most of our daily decisions don't involve the three things the brain cares about. Most of us are very rarely in any real physical danger. Unlike when we were hunter-gatherers, most of us are very blessed to never have to worry about where our next meal is coming from.

And if you're making decisions at work based on sex, you might have an HR problem on your hands.

So when one of those elements isn't at play, the old brain consults the midbrain. The midbrain was the next part of the brain to develop, and it's where we process all our emotions and the nonverbal information we receive from others, and where we get our gut instincts from. Just like the old brain, this is largely a subconscious process—we aren't always aware of why we feel the way we do, but those feelings don't come from nowhere. The midbrain takes advantage of those eleven million pieces of information every single second and delivers us an answer. It just doesn't tell us how it got there. That's why it's so easy to talk yourself out of things your gut is telling you to do—you don't understand the "why" or where it came from.

Here are a few examples of the midbrain in action:

- You get into a fight with your partner, and in the middle of it, you don't remember why you're angry.
- You walk into a meeting room at work and, before anyone has said anything, you just know something is wrong.
- You meet someone and instantly take a liking to them—you "click." The reverse is also true—when you meet someone and you instantly dislike them for no reason at all.

None of those are logical processes, yet oftentimes we find those gut feelings to be incredibly accurate. Sometimes we follow them and sometimes we think our way out of them by trying to understand the "why" behind them.

Finally, we have the new brain. This is the last part of our brain to develop and it's where we consciously process all logic and reason. And this is the part of the brain that gets us into trouble, because unlike the other parts of the brain, we are aware of the work it's doing. That leads us to believe that we are creatures that make decisions based on logic and reason, but the reality is that the old brain (which makes decisions based on survival) and midbrain (which makes decisions based on emotions) have far more power when it comes to decision-making—it's just going on behind the scenes, whereas the processes of the new brain are in the open where we can see them.

Here's what this means: Human beings make decisions emotionally and then justify them rationally. That's true of me, you, your partner, your coworkers, and everyone you know. Unless they are a zombie, every single person you encounter makes decisions emotionally and justifies them rationally. There are no exceptions—it is the way the brain works.

I'm harping on this because there are people who find this very hard to wrap their heads around. We don't want to admit the role that emotions play in almost all of our decisions, both in and out of work. At the end of the day, work is more like high school than we dare to admit—it really does come down to who likes you and who does not. We may not be able to easily explain why we like someone, but when you like someone, it becomes a heck of a lot easier to have a positive experience when you're working with that person.

You see instances every day where this plays out. Think of times when you put together a case for a project or an idea that's grounded in logic, reason, and data. You've got examples of others in the industry who've had success with similar strategies, including competitors. You've done your homework. You know it's a good idea. Yet, when you go to sell it to the boss, they dismiss your work entirely in favor of something they read in an email newsletter that morning.

Here's another one: Think of someone you've worked with that you do not like. Every time this person opens their mouth, you can feel your eyes rolling back in your head. Do you ever fully consider this person's ideas, looking for how they could bring the team success? If you're honest with yourself, the answer is probably no. Emotionally, it's very hard to separate how you feel about someone from the ideas they're expressing. It could be the best, most well-thought-through, logical, rational plan that has ever been presented, and you still probably wouldn't be receptive to it because you don't like them.

BECOME AWARE OF YOUR EMOTIONS

Logic and reason—those are things we're comfortable with. But when you accept that emotions are intrinsically involved in every decision and that you can't eliminate them, the question of what to do with your emotions becomes so much more complicated. Recall strong emotions and suddenly you're flashing back to instances when your parents told you that you would never amount to anything, or when you felt ganged up on or disregarded, or when you had your heart broken for the first time. Some of you will even feel physically uncomfortable reading this chapter because you've pushed your emotions so far down into your subconscious.

Suppressing your emotions because you're not "supposed" to be emotional at work, and the thought of it makes you feel uncomfortable, is the easy way out. I want to challenge you to go the other way: Embrace your emotions. Bring them out of your subconscious into your conscious thought, and then use your awareness of what you're experiencing emotionally to help you create better stories that move you toward your goals.

You see, the problem is not that we have emotions. The problem is when we make judgments based on those emotions without realizing it, and those judgments are what we use to create stories to logically explain what we're experiencing. Here's an example: Your boss hands back a report you spent days on with a ton of red ink. Before you've even read the specifics of their comments, you know they've absolutely ripped your work to shreds. You feel defeated, angry, and inadequate, and start creating stories: Nothing I ever do is right, my work is awful, my boss hates me, I can never win, I'm not good enough. With those stories in your head, think about the actions that will follow: You withdraw; your confidence goes down; you stop offering your ideas because you don't think any of them are good enough; you start checking out from work and just do the bare minimum to get by. Do any of those actions lead to an ideal professional experience? No! At best, you're indifferent. At worst, you're miserable.

When you avoid judgment, you allow every circumstance you find yourself in to be a blessing. Remember, you are in control of the stories that you're creating. When you become aware of your emotions and look at them from a nonjudgmental perspective, it will help you create better stories. So let's change up our scenario a bit: Your boss hands back the ripped-to-shreds report. You still feel those same sad emotions; nothing has changed yet. But this time you stop yourself, take a breath, and look at what's going on from a nonjudgmental perspective. You see that you're angry at your boss because you worked really hard and they didn't acknowledge it. You see that all the edits you've gotten back make you feel like you're not good enough and there's no road to success. But instead of following those emotions, you've detached from them. That allows you to take control and take a different path: "Do those emotions serve me? No. How else could I look at this situation? Well, I know what my boss doesn't like, and I can make changes to the report to give them what they need. In fact, those changes might even make my work better—maybe they know things I don't. They did take the time to read the report and go over it carefully, which is better than ignoring it. It didn't just get thrown on a pile—they gave it time and attention, which means they value my work. Why would they take the time to do all this if they weren't trying to help? Some of these edits make sense, and I'm really glad they caught that typo on page four. It won't take long to make updates at all."

And you're already headed down the road of creating a much better story for yourself, one that serves the experience you want to create rather than putting you in reactive mode in regard to what's been handed to you. None of that would have been possible without your being aware of the warning indicator those initial negative emotions provide you. You see, you haven't eliminated emotions from the equation. Doing that would have made you more or less a work zombie (and no one wants that!). Instead, you viewed the situation from the beautifully detached perspective of a master chess player, which allowed you to reserve your judgment so that you could find your best next move. That left you open to creating a different story—one that allowed you to have a better experience. And when you do this, your emotions about the situation change. You might not feel great about a report being handed back to you with tons of red ink, but you certainly feel better than you did before. Perhaps you even feel optimistic or like your boss did you a favor. Certainly, you see the opportunity for a more successful outcome.

SELF-MASTERY EXERCISE

To understand how to create the stories that best serve your goals, first you have to become aware of what you're shooting for. Take out your journal and ruminate on this question: In my ideal professional experience, what do I want my day-to-day experience to feel like?

Do you want to feel empowered? Confident? Valued? Appreciated? What type of relationship do you want with your boss? Your peers? Your subordinates? How do you want to feel when you walk into the office or when you go home for the night? If you're feeling stuck, Google the term "feeling wheel" and look at the images that come up—those should give you some ideas.

There's no right or wrong answer to this, but what you're doing is creating your bar: The standard you are responsible for holding yourself to. When what you're experiencing on a daily basis does not line up with your standard, that's when you know that you need to stop yourself and change your story.

LISTEN TO YOUR BODY

Being constantly aware of what's going on in your head is exhausting when you first start doing it. It's like a muscle you haven't worked out in years, and all of a sudden you're telling it to lift more weight than it ever has in your life. So it's okay to start small with very basic levels of awareness. Keep it simple and just ask yourself how your body feels when you're in different situations at work. That will tell you a lot about what's going on in your head.

When we're under emotional stress, we feel physical evidence of it. Think of when you have a nightmare. You wake up and you're nervous, you're shaking, you're sweating, your heart is racing, maybe you even feel out of breath. You haven't just run a

5K—you've been soundly asleep in bed. Your body is responding to what is going on in your head. And it works the same way when you're awake. Maybe you have to present in a meeting and your palms start to sweat. You're nervous, afraid of looking like a fool in front of a group of people you want to respect you. Or maybe you're learning that your boss has decided on a strategy that you have fought against, and your whole body starts to tense up—you're angry and you could jump into a frustrated, ill-considered response at any moment.

Start learning more about the emotions at play simply by asking yourself how your body feels. Are you relaxed? Sitting casually with open body language, or do you have your arms crossed in front of your chest in a more closed-off posture? Do you have tension or pain anywhere that isn't injured? Are you shaking or fidgeting? Use whatever is going on as a sign to help you be aware of how you're perceiving the situation. Don't judge it; just observe it and think about what that means for the course of action you're considering and how the people around you might respond to it. The more mental strain you're under, the more likely you're going to default to your innate preferences and tendencies.

REALITY IS SUBJECTIVE

Based on how you know the brain works and the role that emotions play, you may have guessed that the "reality" you experience at work is not an objective experience that everyone looks at and understands in the same way. Instead, "reality" is subjective because we are filtering information through our emotions. Most of the people you work with are not going to do the same work that you just did in the first part of this chapter, so they will continue to be reactive based on their emotions. That means, if they're having a good day, they're going to see things in a more or less positive light. If they're having a bad day, they're going to see the exact same information more negatively. If they like someone, they're going to be more open and receptive to things that person has to say, but if they don't like someone, nothing that person can say or do will be good enough to win them over.

Once you've mastered basic awareness of your emotions, and are able to change your story, it can be useful to understand some of the other tricks your brain plays on you at work. This will allow you to see when you or your colleagues are being driven by emotion so that you can look at the situation and create the story that best serves your goals.

Some of the most common tricks that your brain plays on you at work are projection, confirmation bias, and the fundamental attribution error.

Projection

Projection is the idea that what you see others doing is nothing more than a reflection of the things going on in your own head—insecurities, fears, feelings of not being good enough, memories of past experiences that were painful to you. This occurs when you're not accepting responsibility for how you're feeling because it's easier to put it onto others than to take ownership of it yourself.

Say you meet a new coworker and instantly dislike them. Consciously, there's no logical basis for this dislike—you know the person hasn't said or done anything wrong. Time goes on, and maybe after the initial interaction, they've even gone out of their way to get on your good side. Still, you can't help but come back to your initial impression. Then a disconnect occurs—you feel something but you can't explain it, so you don't want to take responsibility for it. In response, your brain will try to trick you into thinking that it's the other person's fault and give you reasons to believe that it's not you who dislikes them . . . it's the other person who dislikes you! You are projecting your emotions onto them. You'll justify this idea and convince yourself of its truth by reading into the words they say to you, the tone they use, the looks they give you— all things that objectively are probably not good or bad—but you'll find a way to read them with the worst possible intentions so that you have a list of examples that show this person does not like you. This makes you feel okay about not liking them, even though you've invented your justification for it and have created a problem where one may not have existed.

Anytime you're feeling negatively about someone you're working with or a project you're tackling, it can be easy to get into a defensive mode to explain away the negative feelings. Instead, be very deliberate about putting yourself into awareness mode. Picture yourself zooming out and looking at the entirety of the situation, as if you're looking down at a chessboard, observing the pieces to figure out your next move. You're reserving judgment—nothing you see is good or bad. It just is.

Once you're there, consider what you might be projecting onto your current situation. Is it that the person you're dealing with has qualities that remind you of things you don't like in yourself? Is it that you're experiencing impostor syndrome and don't feel like you're good enough to accomplish the goal in front of you? Is it that you've failed at a similar type of project in the past and worry about the same outcome now?

SELF-MASTERY EXERCISE

Whenever we feel negative, stressed out, or anxious about something, it usually comes down to one key emotion: Fear. Fear of failure, loss of control or safety (as a result of job loss and a lack of financial security), etc. The problem is that most of our fears are not real—they are not based in reality. They are simply emotional reactions, and we find ways to project them onto the context we're in and the people we're working with as a means of dealing with them.

Instead, become aware of your fear. If you can dig deep and identify what you're afraid of, you'll be able to solve the problem. Ask yourself, "What am I afraid of?" Whatever your first answer is, dig deep. Peel back the layers. If the answer is that you're afraid the project you're working on will fail, perhaps what you're really afraid of is losing your job and not having financial security, or you're afraid that if the project fails, that means you're not good enough. Or both.

Once you've got your fear identified, look for reasons to contradict it. If you're afraid of losing your job, ask yourself how often your organization fires people, or if you've ever lost a job before. If you're afraid of not being good enough, look for times when you've done amazing work that you're really proud of. Once you have your contradictory evidence, ask yourself if there's really any reason to be afraid here. Most of the time, the answer is no.

Don't be afraid to use this same strategy when you find your colleagues pushing back on ideas. A great question to ask when you encounter resistance is "What are you afraid of?" You'll stop your colleagues dead in their tracks and force them to look at the situation from a new perspective. This usually gets closer to the true issue. From there, you'll be in a better position to find a work-around or a compromise.

Confirmation bias

When I was preparing to start my dissertation, I had to go to a series of workshops led by faculty, and in one of them, the leader remarked, "If you want to do something, you just need to figure out a way to justify it based on things that have been done before. You can justify almost anything."

Think back to when you were in school and had a research report to write. After some work, you come up with a thesis statement that articulates your position on the topic. After you present your thesis, you need to back it up. Do you follow up with data that contradicts your ideas? No! You present the reasons in favor of your idea, not the reasons against it. That doesn't mean that contradictory information doesn't exist—it usually does, but you've weeded it out.

Research papers assume that you've done your homework beforehand and have considered different positions before settling on your thesis. But in the workplace, this type of openness to ideas is atypical. More often, people are operating from a place of preference. Imagine, for example, that one day you decide you like blue pens more than black pens and you want to create a new rule in your department banning black ink. You might use Google to find evidence to support your idea, looking for studies touting the productivity benefits of blue pens, and you'd probably find articles or research to support the notion . . . but you may not look for information that presents data against what you want to do. Welcome to the wonderful world of confirmation bias. What most people will do when they're trying to make a case for something at work is seek out information that supports the idea and avoid information that contradicts it. You don't make a list of pros and cons—

you just find a whole bunch of pros and pretend the cons are nonexistent.

Confirmation bias happens all the time in the modern workplace. People have a very clear position and they seek out information, feedback, and opinions that support that position. We've all been in those meetings where the person in charge says they want to have an open discussion about a particular strategy or initiative, but it's clear from the start of the meeting that they aren't really interested in a discussion. They want people to tell them how great their idea is. If you support their idea, they welcome your feedback openly, nodding their head in agreement as it's presented. But if you present something that contradicts what they want to hear, all of a sudden you're on the outs—not only with them, but with the group of people that have already expressed their approval.

SELF-MASTERY EXERCISE

You can't control if others are engaging in confirmation bias, but you can put checks on yourself to make sure you don't inadvertently do so, and hold yourself accountable to staying open to dissent. Combat your own confirmation bias with projects at work by conducting a "premortem." Here's how it works: You get a group of people in the room before a project has started and you ask them to imagine that you've executed the project . . . and it has been a total and complete failure. Next, you ask them what went wrong in this scenario. Keep an open mind and don't dismiss anything—list out all the possible problems so you can account for them ahead of time. When you first do this, it may seem like a gut punch and bring out all your worst insecurities. However, research shows that this exercise alone will increase a project's chance of success by 30 percent.

People engage in confirmation bias when judgment enters the picture. They judge information that does not overtly support their idea as bad, and the story they're telling themselves is that opposing views or data impair their ability to be successful. But what if information just *is*, with no value or consequence immediately attached to it? Remove the judgment—different views and perspectives are not good or bad. They're just different, like cats and dogs. When you view them dispassionately, you can look at the information and viewpoints in front of you and see where the overlaps and opportunities are. Then you can change the story from "opposing views impair my success" to "diverse viewpoints facilitate my success."

Fundamental attribution error

I have a confession to make: I am a completely unforgiving driver. I have no patience for people who do not understand basic rules of the road like right of way, merging early to prevent a traffic jam, or "don't drive like a slow poke in the fast lane." And if a person makes one of these mistakes while I'm driving in the vicinity, I will cuss them out to no end in the safe confines of my car, where no one can hear me ranting and raving about what a dumb person and horrible driver they might be. Not very zen-like? Well, I'm just human. If swearing by myself in my car is the worst mistake I make, I'm doing alright.

In instances like this, I'm regularly committing the fundamental attribution error. When this is occurring in my car and directed at people whom I will likely never meet in real life, it's okay . . . but if it's directed at people I work with, it can be a big problem. The fundamental attribution error goes like this:

- If you make a mistake, you are more likely to blame environmental factors—things going on around you or circumstances that prevented you from being successful.
- If your colleague makes a mistake, you are more likely to blame it on a fundamental character flaw—"they're incompetent and don't know what they're doing"—completely dismissing any situational factors that might have played a role.

When you commit the fundamental attribution error, you remove your focus from the problem and instead place it on the person, judging their character and experience. You forget that they were put in the job they were for a reason, many times having to go through an extensive hiring and interview process to make sure they had the necessary qualifications. You forget that sometimes people have a bad day or have stressful situations going on in their personal life that you don't know about. You forget that there are decisions made that are simply out of their control, like what the boss has told them to do, or the budget and timeline they're working in.

But it's the future implications you should really worry about. When you make the fundamental attribution error, you aren't doing anything that helps solve the problem in front of you, which means you're detracting from the effort of the team. You're also making judgments about the person in front of you that have a way of sticking around and impacting future interactions. Potentially, you're closing yourself off to the good ideas this person may bring to the table and limiting the type of working relationship you have with them.

Do you want to detract or do you want to support? When you're aware of the impact of the stories you're creating, you put yourself in the position to make the best choice.

SELF-MASTERY EXERCISE

How do you want people to perceive you as a professional? What do you want them to think when your name comes up in conversation? Take out your journal and put some thoughts on paper. If you had complete control to create whatever professional image you wanted, what would it look like?

Once you have some thoughts on paper, you then have to ask yourself how your day-to-day actions support (or detract) from the future vision you want to create. For example, ask yourself if gossiping at work about a colleague being incompetent supports the perception you want people to have of you or detracts from it? Is pointing out someone's shortcomings in a meeting in front of others a key quality of the person you want to be? Hopefully your answers to these questions are no. That's why awareness is so important—all the tricks your brain plays on you are usually things you think without realizing where the ideas are coming from. But now you know, and that means you can take back control and be proactive in creating the experience you want.

YOU CAN'T CHANGE OTHER PEOPLE

Awareness is a mental game. You're bringing what's going on in your subconscious into your conscious and playing with the information in different ways to help achieve your goals. When you start using this type of awareness on yourself, you'll also start looking at your coworkers differently, becoming more aware of why they are doing what they're doing, even if they are not aware of it themselves. And you'll want to help them—show them the light, if you will. We'll work more with how the concepts of awareness apply to your coworkers in later chapters, but for right now, understand this: You cannot change other people. When you try, you are usually asking for trouble. That's not to say that other people can't change—of course they can, if they want to. But that's not your job. Your job is to be aware of what *you're* bringing to the table. When you do that, you will become a model that others can aspire to, and that is the greatest impact you can have on them.

CHAPTER 5

Set Your Goals

We cannot live better than in seeking to become better.

—Socrates

GOAL FOR THIS CHAPTER:

Take control of your workflow, giving it a structure that will keep you focused on your targets, intrinsically motivated, and help you avoid any nonsense distractions.

Goals. You probably have them in your job, though chances are if I asked what goals you're being measured on in your performance review, you would have to give it some serious thought before answering (if you are able to remember at all!). You think about them a handful of times throughout the year, but they don't make a regular, consistent appearance in your everyday workflow. In general, I've found that when I bring up the idea of goals with clients, they experience ambivalence at best and cynicism at worst.

That's about to change. It's time to make the leap from the head game we played in the previous chapters to what you say and do in the office every day. When you zen your work, you start in your head, making sure you are approaching things in a way that embraces your innate gifts and has a higher level of awareness about the stories you're creating. However, if your thoughts don't translate into actions, then what's the point? Your goals are the things that guide your actions. When they're used well, they allow you to weed out the nonsense so that you can focus your energy on what will benefit you the most.

I'm not talking about using goals in the same way that your annual performance review does. I'll be honest: I can count the number of people I've talked to who look forward to the annual performance review on one hand. Employees don't like it—it causes them stress and anxiety, anticipating bad news even though nothing that comes up in the annual review should ever be a surprise. Managers don't like it—they find the process of completing the paperwork something that takes them away from what they'd rather be doing, particularly if they have a lot of people reporting to them. And if you catch an HR professional in a particular moment of honesty, they'll also admit it's one of their least favorite parts of the job because they're always chasing the managers around to do the paperwork! And of course, none of this supports getting work done in a way that drives intrinsic motivation. If anything, it detracts from it.

CHANGE YOUR STORY ABOUT GOALS

We've talked about the difference between being proactive and re-active at work quite a bit. Goals help you to become proactive. Not having goals is like going to the grocery store without a shopping list. Sure, the trip might turn out okay, but you don't set yourself up to come out of the store with what you intended. You forget things, buy stuff you don't need, and get distracted by the latest specials. The same is true at work—when you don't keep a constant eye on your bigger picture, it's a lot easier to get caught up in the non-sense, the politics, and the interpersonal squabbles of the work-place. Your goals are the roadmap that will guide what you do, who you interact with, and what you achieve. When things seem cha-otic around you, you can always revisit and recalibrate your goals to get them back on track. That's why being disciplined with your goals is one of the most impactful things you can do in your career.

SELF-MASTERY EXERCISE

What story are you telling yourself about your goals at work? Take out your journal and write it down. Make sure this feels organic—write the first things that come to mind without judgment. Here are some ideas to get you started: Do you find goals empowering or oppres-sive? Do you think they're a waste of time? Do they help you? How? Are your current goals realistic? Did you feel included in their cre-ation? Use these questions as a jumping-off point to riff on your per-spective. Write without thinking or judging the words that come out on paper.

Once you're done, read your answers over and ask yourself if your current perspective on goals helps you or hurts you in creating an ideal professional experience. If your story supports you in creating

an ideal professional experience for yourself, fantastic! You're ahead
of the game. But if it doesn't, here's the good news: It's your story to
write, or rewrite, as many times as it takes! Consider your current
version a first draft and take a few minutes to write a new story about
how you could look at goals in a way that supports your experience
instead of detracting from it.

Sometimes, when you're changing your story, it can be helpful
to change your language. It doesn't matter what language your organization uses to describe goals—you can use whatever is the
most helpful for you in framing your daily efforts.

For the rest of this chapter, let's differentiate your performance
targets from the personal goals that I'm going to ask you to set.

- The goals your boss sets that you'll be evaluated on are **performance targets**. These are the things, realistic or not, that you're
  going to talk about in your annual performance review and that
  the organization is going to use to decide if you get a promotion
  and a raise. You may or may not have any input in creating these
  targets, and that's okay. We'll work to fix that situation next.
  For now, just view them without passing judgment.
- Your **personal goals**, on the other hand, are created by you to
  help focus your efforts, build and sustain momentum, and create a fulfilling professional experience. But they shouldn't exist
  in a vacuum either—done well, your personal goals will help
  you achieve the performance targets your organization will be
  evaluating you on.

Make sense? The objection I hear most often from people on
setting their own goals is this: "I already have my goals in the

annual review; I can't go outside of it." So, before we get into how to set your personal goals effectively, let's take care of that objection. Of course you can set your own goals! No one is stopping you but yourself. If it helps, just keep your personal goals private at first—you don't need to share your personal goals with anyone or tell people how you're utilizing them to improve your day. That gives you the freedom to put them in a form that is most helpful for you, regardless of whether that's the form used in the annual performance review. At the end of the day, your organization employs you because you fulfill a need for them. If you fulfill that need and you're doing so legally and ethically, most of the time they won't care exactly what process you used to get there.

KNOW WHERE YOU ARE STARTING FROM

With that context in mind, the first thing you need to suss out is what you're actually being measured on at work. Go dig through your performance review files and figure out what you will be evaluated on in your next review cycle. If you can't find it, ask your boss. If they don't know, check with HR. And if you still can't find your performance targets, suggest to your boss that you would like to create them. One of two things is going to happen at that point:

- You'll work with your boss to come up with a list of performance targets.
- They'll say, "That's a great idea!" and then never follow up. If your boss doesn't help you, create your own performance targets. Give them to him or her in your next one-on-one meeting and say, "Here's what I'm thinking about. What do you think?" It'll provide a jumping-off point.

Now, as we've discussed, the list of performance targets you end up with at this juncture may or may not be something you agree with. That's okay. Keep in mind that your organization's goals aren't designed to help you create your ideal professional experience—they're designed to support your leadership's goals and help your organization increase its bottom line. There's nothing wrong with that—it's' just the context you're working in.

So you've got your list of performance targets. The next thing I want you to do is develop your broad personal goals.

SELF-MASTERY EXERCISE

Personal goals are all about where you want to go, but you're not just throwing darts at a map on the wall—you need to know the direction you want to head in. We'll start by looking at your big picture: Let yourself fantasize about what you want your job to be as if you had no boundaries or restrictions. Don't worry about the details yet—we'll drill down into those later.

Fantasize about work? Well, yes. Remember back to when you first applied for, and eventually accepted, your job? Chances are you were excited! It's easy to forget about this honeymoon period once you get bogged down in the day-to-day—it's like the new-car smell wearing off. But think back to that time. What excited you about the job? What did you hope it would be? What made you accept the offer? Going back to the beginning is a great place to start identifying your personal goals because it was a time when all the muck wasn't there yet—the job was still new and shiny, full of possibility and promise.

In the previous chapter, you did an exercise about what you want your daily experience to feel like. Let's build on that. Take out your journal and write a description of your ideal experience at work. Start by asking yourself three simple questions:

- What do I love about my current workday?
- What drives me crazy?
- What do I wish I could spend more time doing?

Use these questions as a jumping off point and let yourself dream about what your work experience could be like. And don't consider this an unrealistic fantasy—you may not be able to snap your fingers and create it instantly, but over time you will be able to make it a reality if you put the work in.

MAKE YOUR GOALS SHORTER

If you've done the exercises up to this point, you've got a ton of information to work with. You know what you want your professional experience to feel like from the previous chapter. You've gotten clarity on the work that enhances your day-to-day experience and what detracts from it. And you know how your organization is evaluating your performance. Now you're going to take that information and create your personal goals.

Let's focus just on your performance targets. The first thing you need to do is to take the targets your organization wants you to hit and break them down into more manageable chunks. Ask yourself what needs to be accomplished every month to hit them all by the time you have your next performance review. Once you've done that, take your monthly targets and break them down by week—if you know where you want to be at the end of the month, you can create targets for week one, week two, week three, and week four. Create a calendar that you can use to track your progress every week. It's best to do this in a digital format because you need to maintain flexibility—some weeks you will achieve your targets and some weeks you won't. Either way, it's okay, but you need to be able to adjust your targets as you go based on the progress you've made.

Breaking down your performance targets like this does a few things. First, it takes big projects that might seem insurmountable as annual goals and suddenly makes them feel achievable. Imagine running a marathon—that's 26.2 miles. It seems like an impossible task. But if you only focus on completing the mile in front of you, rather than thinking about the great length you have to go, it's more doable because the finish line doesn't seem so far away. In fact, it seems really close! And if you celebrate the finish of each mile in the same way that you would when you cross the big finish line at the end, even better. Before you know it, you've run a marathon.

This is what weekly goals do—they allow you to focus on the mile in front of you, right now, celebrating each win along the way. You can see all the moving pieces at play and how little efforts every day lead up to big things. This helps you to build momentum as you go, and momentum is what helps you do big things. When you're trying to move a large object, it's significantly easier to keep it moving once you've started than it is to move it from a stationary position. The more momentum you build, the easier it is to sustain.

Second, looking at the smaller chunks helps you evaluate what resources you need and figure out how to obtain those resources in advance, instead of waiting until the last minute when they may not be available. You aren't operating on an island by yourself in the office—you'll need your coworkers' help and access to resources they have. For example, if you're redoing the company website, then you'll need to work with designers, writers, and programmers to put the pieces together. You'll need to have user testing to make sure what you put out into the world aligns with your intention. You'll likely need a budget to cover any external resources you need. Add this planning into your weekly targets so that you can communicate with the relevant stakeholders ahead of your targets and make sure they're on board. It will give you incredible peace of mind to know the moving pieces are accounted for and ready so you won't be stressing yourself out at the last minute.

Finally, breaking your performance targets down into weekly sprints gives you something to talk about with your manager every week, keeping them updated on the progress you're making and how they can help you remove obstacles as they come up. Make sure you have a regular weekly meeting with them on the calendar, and when you walk into that meeting, take control of it in the following ways:

- Remind them of the performance target(s) you're working toward.
- Outline progress you've made in the previous week.
- Offer next steps—what you'll be working on in the coming week.
- Identify roadblocks that you've hit that your manager can help you navigate. Remember, your success is their success. They have a vested interest in helping you, and most will if they are given very clear direction.

What if your manager doesn't want to meet with you every week or consistently blows off these meetings? That's okay—you're not responsible for them. You're only responsible for yourself. Whether they are coming to the table or not, it is still your job to meet those targets, so you must keep pushing forward. Do your best to make these meetings consistent, but regardless of when they occur, be able to walk in completely prepared. "Here's what

I've accomplished since we last met, here's what I'm currently working on, and here's where I need your help." You can also take advantage of the paper trail that email offers you to send them a weekly update on all of these items if you can't get in front of them in person.

When you report back to your manager on a very consistent basis, you start creating a specific story in their head about you: You are not someone they need to worry about. They don't need to babysit or micromanage you—you're holding yourself accountable for your performance targets; they don't need to do it for you. You're on the ball. You have it together. If there's a problem, you've been communicating with them transparently and they're confident they will hear about it. That's a great story for someone to tell about you, and when it comes time to think about raises and promotions, you'll have set yourself apart from everyone you work with that isn't engaging in this type of consistent communication. Even if you don't meet your targets, they will know you did everything you could to get there. A lot of times, knowing someone is reliable and can be counted on means a heck of a lot more than if you met an arbitrary deadline. It's when you drop the ball or don't plan ahead like you should that your value to the organization really comes into question. Approaching your performance targets in this way creates the impression that you are someone to be relied upon, and in a lot of organizations, that's a rare and extremely valuable commodity. It sets you up to chart your own path.

It's important to keep in mind that all of this should be considered a flexible, fluid process. If you don't meet a weekly target, no big deal—just account for that in next week's goals. If something goes wrong, focus on what you need to do to get back on track. If your boss puts another big project on your plate, accept it without resistance but make sure you communicate clearly what that will mean for your ability to meet your performance targets, and then start the process of breaking your new targets down into weekly sprints. This is not something that you start and end—this is a structure that you'll always need to follow to be successful.

START EVERY DAY WELL

So what happened to all that information about what you want your day-to-day to feel like and what you want to work on? You'll use that to focus the rest of your experience. Chances are that your daily work is made up of more than focused efforts on achieving your performance targets—you have other duties that you're required to do but that don't actually make it into the performance review. Let's call these "other duties as assigned," that wonderful nebulous category that appears on lots of job descriptions that essentially means "stuff we need someone to do, and you're the lucky winner." And, of course, there's the x factor of interpersonal relationships and how your coworkers contribute to, or detract from, the experience you're trying to create.

In the opening of the book, I discussed setting up your day from the moment you wake up in the morning. Make it a personal goal to start your day well, one that you hold yourself accountable to every single day. This goal is just as important as your performance targets because the perspective you come into the office with, and the determination you have to maintain a positive outlook, will dictate the stories you tell yourself. And, as we know, it's those stories that affect your actions.

For example, you could make it a personal goal to set an intention for your day as soon as you wake up: "Today I'm going to feel productive and proud of the progress I'm able to make." It's that simple—no reason to make it any more complex. Then you've got to do whatever you need to do to honor that intention. Most of the time, this is just about being aware of the stories you're creating and doing your best to make ones that serve you. For example, say you're in a meeting and a coworker tries to throw you under the bus on a project you're both working on. In the moment it happens, you might feel as though you failed at something, questioning if your coworker's perceptions of events are accurate. However, now you know enough to realize that they're probably doing it because they feel they've failed and are projecting that failure onto you. Simply make the decision not to allow them to mess with your head. They're saying what they're saying, but so what? If you buy into it, that's just going to give it more legs than it rightfully deserves.

This is where it gets tough, because you need to be highly disciplined about the stories you're creating. But remember that this is about honoring your goals—the decisions you have made. No one forced you to buy this book. No one is going to force you to honor your intentions. If you don't want to, don't! But understand that if you don't, you're not doing your part to create the professional experience you say you want . . . and if you don't do your part, then you can't expect anyone to do it for you. Should your organization make the effort to create an engaging, fulfilling experience for all its employees? Yes, and the ones that do will reap the bottom-line results from it. However, if you don't take personal accountability, then nothing your organization ever does will be enough to help you.

That said, this takes practice—it's not something you'll likely do well when you first start out because it can be really easy to slip back into bad habits. But as with any goal you give yourself, don't judge yourself or beat yourself up if you don't hit it. Doing so will just make you feel bad, which is the opposite of why you're doing this. Instead, just look at it from a beautifully detached, nonjudgmental place and examine what you could have done to meet your intention. Evaluate it as though you're giving advice to a friend and use that information to help yourself do a little bit better tomorrow. And if you don't meet the goal again the next day, so what? You've got another day to try again. You're not receiving judgment from anyone else, so putting that judgment on yourself when you have a virtually unlimited number of work days to try again is a useless exercise. The only way you lose at this is giving up.

DO MORE OF WHAT YOU LOVE...
AND ELIMINATE WHAT DRIVES YOU CRAZY

Take your list of things you love in your day-to-day and compare it to the performance targets you're working toward. In a best-case scenario, there's a ton of overlap between the two. These are the things that you should have been excited about doing when you accepted the job in the first place. But if the gap between the lists is large, then use it as an opportunity to refocus. Have a conversation with your boss, comparing the job description you accepted to what you're doing now, and ask how you can get your work back on track. This is an opportunity to inspire your boss and let them feel your passion for the projects you want to take on. Get them on board with the vision first. "When I accepted this job, here's what I was going to work on, but here's what I spend most of my time on. I'd love it if we could put our focus back on the original goals. Here's the value I'll be able to provide."

Now, chances are that if things have gotten off track, it will take time to refocus. It's not an instant-gratification exercise where change will happen overnight, so don't simply have the expectation that you'll be able to change it by snapping your fingers. You may have to have multiple conversations with your boss to convince them, and you may have to come up with strategies to off-load responsibilities and find resources or staff members to support you. All of these issues are fixable problems as long as you have the patience to let the process play out. Persistence and resiliency will win the day here. Create the story that you're enjoying every minute of it because it's helping you get to where you want to be. If you don't see movement, eventually you'll need to assess whether this is the right company or organization for you. But don't jump right to quitting—give it a chance to play out. If you're consistently meeting your performance targets, communicating transparently, and creating the story in your boss's head that you are an invaluable resource, you'll be surprised at how flexible they can become.

In the meantime, see what you can include in your day from your "love" list. Chances are there are smaller projects you can take on, or initiatives you can champion, or passion projects you can cultivate that will fill the gap while you're figuring the rest out.

And finally, that list of things that drives you crazy. If you're honest with yourself, most of the things that are on that list are probably a result of the story you're telling yourself about them. Tell yourself a different story (for example, "These things are easy obstacles to jump over to achieve my goals") and you've eliminated 90 percent of your list. Well done! That's huge progress already.

But of course, there are parts of your job that aren't going to be your favorite things to do—that's the reality of any job you come across. First, accept it. It's not good or bad . . . it's just part of the job! Next, make sure the work you don't like doesn't get in the way of the work you love. A way you can account for this is to structure your workflow well. At the beginning of the week, take the things you don't like doing and block your time in a way that allows you to get them all done and out of the way. The task is out of the way and you've freed up the rest of your week to focus on your performance targets and do work you love.

CELEBRATE YOUR VICTORIES—ALL OF THEM

This last part is really important. Anytime you achieve one of your personal goals or performance targets, big or small, celebrate the hell out of it. Somewhere along the line, we got the impression that celebrations have to be reserved for the big things, like birthdays and graduations, that happen rarely. How absurd! Every day can be a celebration if you allow it to be, and the more celebrations you have, the better your work experience will be. Whenever you meet any of your goals, take a moment to give yourself a pat on the back and enjoy the small victory. Allow yourself the momentum that will carry you to the next goal and beyond.

CHAPTER 6

Become Unapologetically Optimistic

Let us learn to appreciate there will be times when the trees will be bare, and look forward to the time when we may pick the fruit.

—Anton Chekhov

GOAL FOR THIS CHAPTER:

Discover how you can be your own coach and embrace an optimistic outlook in any situation you find yourself in.

Four years ago, a friend of mine was diagnosed with adult Wilms cancer. She was thirty-one years old and after being misdiagnosed twice for a UTI, a doctor at urgent care finally had the good sense to send her for a CT scan. They found a giant tumor on her kidney. Two weeks later she had surgery to remove both the tumor and her kidney before starting six months' worth of chemotherapy. But none of this is what I remember from witnessing her journey—what I remember is that I saw a constant stream of photos on her Facebook account of her with a giant smile on her face. And when she was in the hospital before and after surgery, at her chemo appointments, trying on all sorts of wigs with different colors and styles. When her hair started to fall out, she purposefully cut it into a mullet just so she could take hilarious pictures of herself holding a can of Pabst Blue Ribbon with a cigarette in her mouth. She even shaved her head before getting her oncologist's permission because she was so excited about being bald. Anyone going through this experience at such a young age would have a lot to be angry about . . . but she never expressed anything but absolute unapologetic optimism. Today, thankfully, she's cancer-free.

When you compare your experience at work to something like fighting and surviving cancer, it all seems so small and petty, doesn't it? You know this conceptually—unless you are a health-care professional or in the military, your job is probably not a question of life or death. Yet it's so easy to let the little things that go on in the office every day get to you. But when you see someone stare down cancer before she's even old enough to have had a mid-life crisis, it emphasizes the reality that being happy and optimistic is not a reflection of the circumstances you find yourself in. It is a choice.

We all know those people who come into the office and are happy and have a great attitude no matter what gets thrown at them. They never seem to get stressed out or overwhelmed. Sometimes people think they are just looking at the world through rose-colored glasses, but that's not what's going on at all. They're not ignoring all the problems that exist—they simply choose not to let them disrupt their attitude. For some, this seems to come easier—more naturally—than for others. But anyone, regardless of innate disposition or work style, can do the same thing if they make the choice to do so. It's both the easiest and most difficult choice one could ever make. The act of deciding on its own is simple—you put your stake in the ground and commit to an optimistic direction. It's the follow-through that becomes difficult. When you're first learning how to do it, choosing to be optimistic no matter what can feel like it requires you to get knocked down and get back up, over, and over, and over again, knowing that every time you get back up, you're closer to creating the experience you want. The secret is that once you master unapologetic optimism, you're better able to roll with the punches, and what previously knocked you down won't even faze you.

OPTIMISM IS NOT THE ABSENCE OF CHALLENGES

Let's get philosophical for a moment. I want to make an analogy involving color—specifically, black and white. Generally speaking, we associate black with darkness or bad things in the world—anger, hatred, depression, demons, etc. White is the opposite of black and we associate it with all the good in the world—positivity, purity, goodness, heaven (if you believe in that). In other words, black bad, white good.

So, for our purpose here, I want you to associate all the things you don't like about your professional experience with the color black—anything that causes you stress, anxiety, fear, or anger. And associate all the things you like with the color white—coworkers who make you happy or whom you enjoy, getting told "great work" or "thank you," being excited about starting a new project, etc.

SELF-MASTERY EXERCISE

Take out your journal and draw a line down the middle of one of the pages. Label one column "black" and the other "white." Create a list of everything that makes you feel bad at work in the black column, and everything that makes you feel amazing in the white column.

These things can be specific to the job you're currently in (e.g., "I hate my boss—he sets unrealistic goals that stress me out") or they can be more generic (e.g., "I love working on my own without distraction. It helps me focus"). If you're having a hard time thinking of things for your white column, it can be useful to look at the opposite of what you wrote in the black column—if you know what you don't like, then it's an indicator of what you would like.

A lot of people are confused about the origin of black and white, thinking that black represents all colors in the rainbow and white represents the absence of color. It may seem counterintuitive, but the opposite is actually true—black is the absence of color and white is every color you can think of put together. What happens when you take black (no color) and add white (all the colors) to it? It becomes less black.

To say this another way: A black experience just lacks the presence of white.

Think about what this means in terms of your experience at work: When you add positivity and optimism to a negative situation at work, it inherently makes it a little less black. The more white you add, the less black it gets. Take something on your black list and think about the story you've created around that item. Let's look at the example from the self-mastery exercise—my boss sets unrealistic goals. That could create a really negative (black) story:

- Unrealistic goals cause me stress and anxiety.
- When my boss sets unrealistic goals, he wants me to fail.
- Unrealistic goals mean I have no chance of being successful. I'm going to be a failure.
- If I fail, I could lose my job.

What happens when you take that black experience and add white to it? Suddenly, your whole story starts to change:

- Goals I think are unrealistic are stressful . . . but sometimes a little stress can be a good thing. I've had projects where I work better with pressure than without it.
- I don't know how I'm going to achieve them now . . . but so what? That doesn't mean they're impossible. It just means I haven't figured out the way there yet.
- My boss doesn't want me to fail—he just wants to challenge me to push myself to the next level.
- If I meet these goals, that could mean a big promotion.

Based on those two stories, which one will support the professional experience you want to create? We've started from exactly the same place, but the person who chooses to go down the path of the first story is going to have a very different experience than the person who chooses to go down the path of the second story. And look, maybe the person in the second story doesn't meet the goals they were being pushed to . . . but they're going to get a heck of a lot closer than the person who comes into work every day with an "I can't do it" attitude. People who bring cynicism and pessimism to work with them rarely achieve the type of success they are capable of.

FAKE IT TILL YOU MAKE IT

Everything you do every moment of every day contributes to creating your experience. If you want an experience that feels productive, engaging, and motivating, you have to bring it—being unapologetically optimistic is part of the deal you make because every time you bring anything less, you should expect to create a less fulfilling experience. Give less and you'll get what you should expect based on your contribution.

Conceptually, this is easy to understand. But putting it into practice in the real world is a bit harder because it's not like flipping a light switch. Over the course of our lives, our experiences train us to give more weight to possible negative outcomes than positive ones. When that happens, fear can take over—fear of losing your job, of failure, of losing control, etc. When fear hits us, either consciously or subconsciously, that's when we react with a fight-or-flight response—we either run away from the problem or we try to fight it aggressively. Unapologetic optimism provides a third option, but it's not one that most people come to naturally. You'll need to consciously redirect yourself from where your mind wants to take you to a path that's better for you to go down.

You may not have been overtly negative in the past, but even the leap from biting your tongue to overtly expressing an optimistic outlook to your coworkers can be a big deal! All this means that it may feel incredibly weird and inauthentic when you first try it. But sometimes when you're trying to build a new habit that pushes you outside of your comfort zone, your best course of action is to fake it until it starts to feel comfortable. You're training yourself to do something new, just like when you learned to ride a bike and had to have training wheels while you built confidence. It takes time and practice to learn, but eventually it becomes second nature and the training wheels come off.

SELF-MASTERY EXERCISE

When you're starting to embrace unapologetic optimism, it can be helpful to find a role model—one of those people who always seems to have a smile on their face and a nice thing to say, no matter what. Then, when you find yourself on the verge of making a snarky comment, just ask yourself what that person would do.

Take out your journal and write down the name of your optimism role model. Then take a look back at the black list you made in the previous exercise. Pick an item off it and write about how your role model would approach the situation. You could even give them a call and ask them! Take them out to coffee and say, "I'm curious about how you would handle this situation." They'll probably be flattered that you've reached out in the first place! And then they'll shower you with valuable advice you can use to inform how you move forward in your day.

EMBRACE THE COLLECTIVE EXPERIENCE

One of the biggest objections I get to the unapologetic optimism strategy is this: "What about when things go wrong? Or my work is criticized? Or my budget doesn't get approved? Or Johnny Jones from marketing throws me under the bus?" And my answer is always the same, regardless of the specific scenario: Find the blessing.

Oftentimes, hindsight will allow you to look back at less-than-ideal situations over the course of your life and see that they worked out for the best. Your flight gets delayed . . . and you meet an amazing business contact at the airport bar. You lose your job . . . but you get an even better one. The boyfriend you're head-over-heels for breaks up with you to date your best friend . . . and you meet the perfect guy right afterward (and didn't invite either of them to the wedding!).

Those who embrace the unapologetically optimistic philosophy are able to look at what they have in front of them in the present moment and see it for all of its potential rather than focusing on the things that they don't like. When the boyfriend breaks up with you under scandalous circumstances, you could focus on feeling sorry for yourself, lock yourself indoors, and eat several pints of Ben & Jerry's . . . or you could acknowledge that he wasn't good enough for you anyway, and go out and find someone who is. In the unapologetically optimistic case, you're embracing the breakup as a necessary part of finding the right guy.

At work, it is no different. The things that aren't so great are not the end of your story—they're just part of the process. When they occur, remind yourself of all the instances you can look back on and see that they led you to achieve more. If it happened in all those circumstances—most of the time, when you weren't even trying—imagine what you could do when you put your mind to it.

Being unapologetically optimistic does not mean that negative or stressful things don't happen to you at work. It simply means you're allowing that optimism to shine through in the context of stressful experiences rather than choosing to focus on the worst possible outcome. Remember, white is the presence of all colors, including the darker ones. Those darker colors will always be there. You can't get rid of them. Focusing on the fact that less-than-ideal things happen at work does you no good—it doesn't reduce your stress, or help you be more productive or successful. In fact, it does just the opposite. Creating the experience you want requires you to make the choice between hanging on to the angst or embracing the obstacles and setbacks in front of you as part of your path to success. Thomas Edison knew this. When he was inventing the lightbulb and went through unsuccessful prototype after unsuccessful prototype, he famously quipped that he hadn't failed—he'd just found ten thousand ways that don't work.

It's judgment about the things that seem to throw your work off track that gets you in trouble. Remove the judgment and suddenly the goal of embracing unapologetic optimism becomes a lot more attainable. The problem comes when people let no be the end of the story. Some of your coworkers might say this is being "realistic." They dwell on all the things—big and small—that they perceive to have gotten in their way of achieving success. Understand that this isn't realism—it's resistance. They have a wall up around them that keeps out any perspectives that might turn a negative into a positive, delegitimizing positive points of view before giving them a moment's consideration.

That's not to say you can't take a moment to look at things critically or vent when something doesn't go the way you would have liked it to. But let it be just that—a moment. Tell yourself that you're going to give yourself ten minutes to be annoyed and eat your Ben & Jerry's, and then it's time to move on. Your coworkers who are expressing their "realistic" points of view aren't doing that—they're not allowing optimism to shine through in the face of a challenge.

You can't control their actions, and it's pointless to even try. But, as you know, you can control yourself. Many of us have walls up that prevent us from fully embracing an unapologetically optimistic approach. Those walls have been built by people who let us down or who told us that we're not good enough; failures we've had and don't want to repeat; and any number of negative things we've experienced in the course of our careers—like losing a job or working in toxic environments where we were mentally and emotionally put through the ringer. When you discover where your walls are, you'll be better equipped to knock them down when they don't serve you.

SELF-MASTERY EXERCISE

Everyone has negative experiences over the course of their career that stick with them for a long time. Take out your journal and write about the experiences that have impacted you the most. This will help you discover where your walls are.

   This is a tough exercise to do, but it's necessary to discover the things that are influencing your experience today. If you're not feeling emotional when you do it, then you're not digging deep and really considering your triggers. The work will be worth it—when you become aware of what's influenced you in the past, that will allow you to keep it in its proper context so that it doesn't hold you back in the future.

DISRUPT YOURSELF

Once you're aware of your triggers, you'll be better equipped to identify when they are rearing their ugly head in your current context. You've got to be your own best coach in this regard. If you're feeling stressed out, angry, or apprehensive about an idea, try asking yourself these disruptive questions to get your perspective back on track:

- How am I framing this situation? What story am I telling?
- How could I look at this situation differently? How can I make the story more positive?
- How could this turn out successfully? How have similar situations been successful before?
- Do I have any evidence that this won't work out? Do I have evidence that it will?
- How important is this? What's the impact?
- What am I really afraid of?

Usually, you can simply think through these questions in your head, though it can be helpful to write them out in a journal, just like you are doing for our self-mastery exercises. Physically writing things out sometimes spurs new thoughts or revelations that you wouldn't have had otherwise.

This exercise will help you look at whatever context you find yourself in from this more detached perspective, so you can make a decision by taking things in from the point of view of an observer, handling each situation from a more optimistic perspective. It's about having the presence of mind, awareness, and discipline to look at whatever is put in front of you in the best possible light. That, in turn, will allow you to move forward in the way that benefits you the most.

EXPRESS YOURSELF

Being unapologetically optimistic is more than a head game. The real magic happens when other people start to feel your optimism. To get them to feel it, you need to express it.

Expressing an unapologetically optimistic point of view seems simple: You just need to say it out loud. Imagine you're in a meeting and one of your "realistic" coworkers is listing off all the reasons why an idea on the table will never be successful. In your head, you know he's looking at it in the worst possible way—you've asked yourself your disruptive questions and used them to find a way this idea could be a great thing. It does no one any good if you keep those ideas to yourself. Say them! Express your point of view. That's when you start to have real impact, because you're not just creating a better work experience for yourself—you're doing it for the people around you. And in the process you're going to find a whole new batch of workplace allies that you may not have known about before, who are optimistic but feel like they're the only ones in the room.

So why don't people speak up? Because when you do, you often face opposition in the form of all your "realistic" coworkers who make you feel as though you have no business expressing your point of view. This is where optimism becomes unapologetic. You have to look them in the eye and stand your ground. Own your perspective and do not give an inch, even when that little voice in the back of your head starts to scream at you to back down. Here's a secret: Most people question themselves when they put a stake in the ground in front of others (unless they're a legit narcissist, a disorder that leads one to create a made-up world in which they can't do anything wrong). The little voice of doubt is louder for some people than it is for others, but it's always there. The most successful people simply learn to quiet that voice down.

So they push back on you. So what? Your ability to embrace unapologetic optimism doesn't hinge on the words and reactions of others. This is where being beautifully detached is your best friend—you don't need people to agree with you in order to stand your ground, confident that regardless of which way the final decision goes, being optimistic will do more to help you create the experience you want than giving into cynicism will. If people agree with you, great! If they don't, that's fine too, because that's part of the process of achieving success. No harm, no foul. You just need to try again, or find a different way to get there. Expressing anger or stress won't help you. Planning your next step will.

Here's something to keep in mind about the "realistic" coworkers you're standing up against: They keep expressing the same cynical points of view over and over again, in meeting after meeting, because they can. No one stands up to them, and that's how they exert power. It's so much easier to shoot down ideas than it is to support them. If you successfully shoot them down, that means you don't have to do anything to make them a reality and you can continue with business as usual. But supporting an idea . . . that has consequences! It means you're going to have to help—or lead—it to become a reality. When you're making the choice to embrace unapologetic optimism, you're choosing to spend your time at work doing something that might require you to push yourself outside your comfort zone instead of resting on your laurels and doing the same old thing or nothing at all. Anytime you hear someone complaining that a coworker is "afraid of change," what they're really looking for is someone to embrace doing things in a way that pushes your organization past what it's done before. Unapologetic optimism opens the door for you to be that person.

MAKE SOMEONE ELSE'S DAY

One of the easiest ways to get started with unapologetic optimism is simply to make your coworkers feel really great by handing out compliments and high fives like they are going out of style. Most people don't receive nearly enough praise or positive recognition for their efforts at work, and though their boss should be the one providing that kind of reinforcement, there's nothing stopping you from doing it. Compliments are free, they take next to no time to give out, and, when they're given genuinely, they instantly have an impact on the recipient. The person you're speaking to could be having a horrible day, facing challenges you have no idea about, and a few simple words from you can turn it around.

On its own, it's a wonderful thing to do. But the person you're giving the compliment to isn't the only one receiving the benefit. When you give out a compliment to someone else, you're receiving a psychological boost from the altruistic act. Not only will you feel great in the moment, but you'll also get long-term benefits when you do it on an ongoing basis—you'll be happier and more motivated, bring down your levels of stress and susceptibility to depression, and you may even get hit with fewer bouts of colds or the flu. You'll also get the social benefits—your coworkers will trust you more, go out of their way to help you, and (of course!) be more likely to compliment you in return!

CONSISTENCY IS KEY

Anytime you're trying to build a new habit, it generally takes about thirty days of consistent effort. Everything you do every moment of every day either enhances your experience or detracts from it. Create a thirty-day challenge for yourself to help you get through it. Get a print calendar—you can buy one or just print one off from the internet—and make it a goal to do three things every day at work:

- Ask yourself at least one disruptive question. This could be while you're working with others, or just working on a task by yourself that you're struggling with.
- Express optimism about an idea, strategy, project, vision, etc. . . . with at least one other person in the room. Don't overthink this—it could be as simple as saying "I think that's a great idea."
- Give someone you work with a genuine compliment.

Each of these acts takes just a few minutes of time and can be integrated with the day-to-day work you already have. If you can check off most of the boxes on most of the days, by the end of the month, being unapologetically optimistic will become more instinctual and a more integrated part of your experience.

PART III

interacting
with others

Once you've got your head in order, it's time to share your new perspective with the people you see at work every single day. By now you know that your work experience is not dictated by the people you work with, but they're an inescapable factor in reaching your personal goals. You have to make sure the connections you make at work enhance your experience instead of detract from it. Recognizing your coworkers' humanity will help you get there.

In this section, you'll learn how to build amazing relationships with your colleagues; approach each new task, project, and idea with a beginner's mind; boost your confidence; and create new strategies for working with the most difficult people.

CHAPTER 7

Build Amazing Relationships

I believe that every single event in life happens in an opportunity to choose love over fear.

—Oprah Winfrey

GOAL FOR THIS CHAPTER:

Understand the major ways you can have influence in your organization and why relationships are your magic bullet.

t happened when I was twenty-seven years old, right after I got promoted to a director-level position for the first time. Having the title of director was something I had strived toward for years, telling myself that when I attained it I would finally be able to have the type of influence I wanted. To move up the hierarchy, I had been following someone else's lead, whether or not I agreed with it. I knew I had good ideas and that my instincts were usually spot on . . . I just didn't have the position that allowed me to chase those ideas.

And then one day it happened—the company's CEO told me she was making me a director. The feeling when you hit a big career milestone is amazing—it's joy, satisfaction, validation, and relief all rolled into one. I felt like I was on top of the world. All those years of extra hours and hard work had finally paid off. I couldn't wait to start doing what I had been dreaming about, so I hit the ground running. I hired a team of people whom I trusted, I started implementing ideas I had worked on with the CEO, and I built my identity around the fact that I was a director in this company. Things were going great. I had everything I ever wanted . . . or so I thought.

Me, me, me. That was the problem. I was so focused on me, and my title, and my responsibilities, and my team, and my being a "thought leader" that I didn't consider how I was making the people around me feel. In particular, I didn't consider how I was making another director who had been at the company longer than I had feel. I neglected to consider that she had a more grounded relationship with the CEO than I did. I ignored the signs that she was feeding the CEO information that may or may not have had a basis in reality to make herself look good and to make this new, young upstart look bad.

And then the focus on myself, rather than on others, came back to bite me. A little over a year after being put in the role, I was summarily pushed out of it and the team I had recruited and built was given to the other director. I watched from afar as a woman who wasn't as talented or driven as I was took the team I had recruited and continued to do grossly mediocre work with them. But the quality of the work didn't matter—what mattered was that the CEO liked working with her more than she did with me.

I could say it came with no warning because, at the time, I was shocked. But the fact was that I had all the warning signs I needed. I was just ignoring them because I didn't think they mattered. You see, I thought that quality of work was what counted—that if I just had a great output, I would be successful in the role. I didn't realize that your title, or being an expert and a thought leader, doesn't mean anything if you don't have good relationships with the coworkers who have the ability to make or break your work, or who influence those in positions of power. Remember back to what you learned in chapter 4 about how people make decisions—they do it emotionally and then justify them rationally. Quality of work is a rational decision (and a subjective one at that!). Relationships are an emotional connection. Emotion trumps logic and reason every single time.

This is the point that's missed time and time again in career development courses—they talk about networking for the sake of knowing people in your industry and being able to get that next job, but they don't talk about its importance in your day-to-day.

This is not a brand-new concept. There's a famous study from the Carnegie Foundation from 1918 that found that 85 percent of your career success depends on your soft skills—your likability, attitude, and ability to communicate well with others. Only 15 percent depends on your technical knowledge about how to do the job you're being paid to do. One hundred years later, that still remains true because that is how our brains are hardwired. You can't control the subjective judgments people make about you, and you may not even think about them, but you must acknowledge that's the context you're navigating in professionally.

Creating your ideal professional experience is as much about how you bring others into it as it is about your individual self-mastery. That's not to say that you should allow people to dictate your mood or change your perception of yourself. But when it comes to getting things done, sooner or later you're going to need their help, their influence, their resources, and their relationships with others in your organization. This is what trips so many people up—if only you could work on an island by yourself, creating your ideal professional experience would be the easiest thing in the world! Get other people involved, and sometimes it seems like all the hard, independent work you've done can go right out the window. Suddenly you're questioning everything you thought you knew about yourself—your expertise, experience, and value— leaving you with a massive case of impostor syndrome.

No one likes office politics because it's gotten a really bad rap as something people utilize to unfairly get things they don't deserve. But at its core, office politics is just about building amazing relationships with the people you work with. People who play politics well are masters of the relationship game. That's not unfair—that's strategic. They're using the resources they have to create the experience they want! Instead of pooh-poohing it, you can do the exact same thing.

WHY RELATIONSHIPS ARE YOUR GOAL

The mistake I made way back when was that I thought my title— the fact that I was a director—was the be-all and end-all of organizational influence. I had a nice fancy title, so others would have to listen to me. Looking back now, I want to slap the younger version of myself upside the head and say, "What on earth are you thinking?!" It wasn't as though I did anything bad or cruel in my tenure in that role—I've had bosses do much worse. But because I was in a constant state of trying to prove that I could deliver results, I pissed off a lot of people around me without intending to, thinking it was okay because it wasn't personal—it was just business.

Today, I would sit my past self down and give her a stern talking to about the three major types of influence a person can have in an organization: Title, expertise, and relationships. The three are not mutually exclusive—your best-case scenario is being well-rounded in all three areas!

Title

Influence based on your title relates strictly to the organizational chart—whom you report to, who reports to you, whose annual performance review you fill out, and whom you can fire. It's easy to think that this is the most powerful type of influence because the org chart provides a very clear order of rank. Some MBA textbooks even call this type of influence "legitimate power." However, this is actually the weakest of all the influence types we'll look at. Why?

- If influence is strictly by the org chart, that means it limits your sphere to your direct reporting line.
- It makes it difficult to effectively influence the people above you who may hold the purse strings.
- It takes a long time to change. Some people can angle for a promotion for years without result.

When you default to your title as the source of your influence, you limit your impact in so many ways! In your ideal professional experience, you probably need people from across your organization on your side, something you will never achieve based on title or org chart alone.

130 ZEN YOUR WORK

Expertise

Influence based on your expertise allows you to expand your scope beyond your direct reporting line. You can do this when you are perceived to be an expert in something the organization values. That particular skill may or may not be directly related to your current role. For instance, you may be in a marketing role, but you're really great at creating efficient processes, inside and outside of the marketing function. In this case, your influence comes more from an operations perspective than a marketing one.

There's one key word at play here: *Perception*. You can be an expert in something, but if you're not perceived to be one by the people you work with, then you can't influence in that area. And, on the flip side, you can be perceived to be an expert in something that is really not your forte.

Most people can relate to the nightmare of having a boss who has no idea what he or she is doing. I sure can. I was in one of the best jobs I ever had in a professional services firm. I loved the people I worked with and they were excited by what I was bringing to the table. It wasn't glamorous at all, but it was a scrappy organization where entrepreneurship was encouraged.

And then one day my boss decided to hire *her*. I begged him not to. I knew from the minute I interviewed her that she had no idea what she was walking into. Very nice lady, but her knowledge was about twenty years out of date. But she was a friend of a friend and allegedly had built teams in other organizations, and so she came on board as my new boss. She lived up to exactly what I expected of her, but I wasn't the one she was trying to influence. I may not have perceived her to be an expert . . . but the guy who had the power to hire her did. Who knows where the perception came from—the recommendation from a friend he trusted or his lack of understanding of what the job required or current standards. Perhaps she just talked a great game in her interview with him. Regardless, the why doesn't really matter. What matters is that the perception existed. My boss perceived she was an expert so he put her in a position above me because she was able to influence him in a way that I could not.

That's the tricky thing about influence based on expertise—you have to control the perception. The shortcut to that is to build relationships.

Relationships

I once got into a debate with a CEO about a question on an employee engagement survey. It was in the section regarding how the person feels about their boss, and I wanted to include an agree/disagree to the following statement: "I like my boss." The CEO pushed back on this—she thought it should be "respect" instead of "like." But I stood my ground and argued that if we agree that people make decisions emotionally and justify them rationally, we had to ground the question in emotions. Respect is not an emotion. In fact, many times when we use the word *respect* at work, we don't even use it in a positive context. "With all due respect, but . . ." "I respect you, but . . ." The word *respect* misses the mark because it doesn't hit on what really matters in the manager-employee relationship—the likability factor. And it's not just important for managers—it's true at all levels and of all workplace relationships you have.

That's what relationships are—when you like the other person. I'm not suggesting that you have to become best friends with everyone you work with, but that a base level of rapport has to be there. You will enjoy a better working relationship with someone who believes that you have their back, and you feel like they have yours. The more people like you, and the better the relationships you have, the better your experience at work will be. Think about it:

- Do you do favors for people you don't like?
- Do you support projects when they're championed by someone you don't like?
- Do you share resources with people you don't like?
- Are you likely to give a glowing performance review to someone you don't like?
- Are you going to go above and beyond the call of duty to help out someone you don't like?

If you're honest with yourself, then the answer to all those questions is either "no" or "very rarely." If you want to create an environment where people do those things for you, then you have to offer an environment where they can expect you to return the favor. That's what a relationship is when it's functional and healthy—each person in it offers a relatively equal amount of energy to the other. All the questions in the list above are simply about energy. You don't want to take from others more than you are giving to them, just like you don't want them taking from you more than you're receiving in return.

It all comes down to a very simple question: Do you want to come into work every day and work with a group of enemies or be surrounded by a group of friends? You could argue that you don't need to like a person to have a good working relationship with them, and on some level that's true. It's just much, much easier if people like you. I dare say it even becomes a joyful experience, because when you're working with people you like and genuinely want to support, and you get to play a role in their success, there's nothing better.

SELF-MASTERY EXERCISE

What type of influence do you currently have in your organization? Take out your journal and draw three columns on a piece of paper, labeling them "title," "expertise," and "relationship."

- In the title column, list people who report directly to you through a hard-line reporting structure.
- In the expertise column, list people who regularly come to you to ask for your opinion or advice.
- In the relationship column, list the people who you regularly shoot the breeze with, those who come to you for help, and those whom you know you can go to when you're in a bind.

Work with people who can be in more than one column? That's okay! You can have influence over someone in more than one way . . . and the more, the better!

BUILDING STRATEGIC RELATIONSHIPS

Armed with your current sphere of influence, it's time to get strategic with relationship building at work. In an ideal world, you want to proactively build a working relationship with as many people in your office as possible, because you never know when you're going to need to ask someone for a favor when an unexpected project or task comes up. Building relationships is something you want to do ahead of time, so that they are in good shape when you need to use them.

You may think this paints work relationships as purely transactional, because you're making sure you've greased the wheels. In some respects, that's true. But is that a bad thing? It's simply the way of the world—we're more apt to do things for people we like, rather than people we either don't like or don't know at all. If you think about it, all relationships are transactional, with each person in it experiencing a benefit. For example, in my relationship with my husband, I not only get love and companionship with someone whom I genuinely enjoy, I also get someone who cleans the kitchen and who remembers to feed our dogs. In return, he gets someone who plans really fun vacations and goes out of her way to buy him hard-to-find Rubik's Cubes. So the relationship is both personally enjoyable and transactional.

Think about your relationships with your partner, your loved ones, and your friends—there should be elements of give and get involved. That's what makes them healthy and functional. When it comes to work, your relationships will be as emotionally fulfilling as you allow them to be. They can bring happiness, joy, and a feeling of belonging when you allow them to—all wonderful, beneficial things that will contribute to your professional experience and go beyond finishing projects and meeting goals. But at the very least, your relationships at work should give you access to resources (time, energy, budget, staff, etc. . . .) when you're willing to give your own resources in return. Some folks call this "office politics" and view it in a negative light, but if you remove judgment and become an observer in the situation, you'll see that reciprocity is simply fair play.

Building relationships can take time, and when you're getting started, it's a good idea to look at the process strategically.

SELF-MASTERY EXERCISE

Consider your list of performance targets from chapter 5. Take out your journal and write each of your high-level targets on the top of a separate page. Now use the body of that page to brainstorm what resources you'll need to hit or exceed those targets.

Next ask yourself who in the organization can help you get access to those resources. Those people may be in your department or outside of it. Perhaps you need support from folks in the marketing or sales units, input from the program manager, administrative help from the office manager, or a budget from the COO.

Compare the list of people you'll need to bring in to meet your performance targets with the sphere of influence you created in the previous exercise. If you're going to need someone who isn't on your first list, that's where you start strategically building your relationships.

But strategic relationship building goes beyond what you need right now. Think beyond utility—"I need something and this person has it"—and move toward the big picture. Every organization has a finite amount of resources—at some point, there's just no more money/time/staff to be found. So in a very real sense, you are competing against everyone else for your share of that resource pot. The mistake people make is fighting on their own—taking the weight of the world on their shoulders. Instead, what if you teamed up with people who are running in the same direction, with similar goals? There's no use in fighting each other for the same resources if you want the same things.

SELF-MASTERY EXERCISE

Take a look at the list you made in the previous exercise of people you need to build relationships with and think about the goals each of them is working toward. Whose goals align with yours? Who can you share resources with to achieve an end result that is desirable for both of you? These are your work allies.

By now, you should have a good list of people whom you need to build relationships with. Some of these people will probably be quick wins—you generally work well with them, and they with you. But some of them you may not like, or you may have had conflict with them in the past. Regardless of where you're starting from, you can build relationships with anyone as long as you put the past behind you, exist in the present moment, and keep an unwavering focus on what you want to achieve. That means you don't avoid doing the hard things, like creating relationships with people you don't personally enjoy. You do the hard things because they serve the experience you want to create.

For the remainder of this chapter, we'll explore ways for you to build those relationships, regardless of your starting point.

RELATIONSHIPS ARE ABOUT CONNECTION

In 2014, I accepted a job at a public radio station. I had been running my consulting practice on the side for a few years and knew I wanted to do it full time at some point in the near future, but this opportunity was just "too good" to pass up—I had been enamored with public radio for years, and to be a part of it seemed like a dream come true. So I compromised, accepting the job but telling them they were only going to get a few years out of me because I was going to do Zen Workplace full time.

Little did I know that accepting that job would solidify the importance of the work I do now, because it was easily the most toxic place I have ever worked. I left every day feeling angry, frustrated, and unsupported because the narcissism of the person running the organization had trickled down over the course of years into her top staff members—the people I interacted most with. Every day was like being a punching bag, and I can remember very few experiences in my career when I felt so alone.

There was one person in particular that I had to work with a lot—a director of another department. We couldn't have been more different—I perceived him to be the old curmudgeon, and he perceived me to be the young girl who didn't get it. We would constantly pick at each other passive-aggressively in meetings, making comments here and there that weren't intentionally trying to get under the skin of the other but certainly did.

Then one day, it exploded. We were in a meeting with half a dozen other people in the room and we were doing the same thing we always did—pick, pick, pick, pick—and suddenly he just unleashed on me, screaming in the middle of the meeting, in front of other people. To say I was pissed would have been the understatement of the century—I was so angry I couldn't even bring myself to speak, and I just sat there glaring at him for the remainder of the meeting. As soon as it was done, I got up, stormed out of the building, and went to one of my favorite comfort food places—Buffalo Wild Wings (it was boneless wing Thursday!). So I got my boneless wings and a very large beer and I sat there until I was good and ready to go back.

Unfortunately, the time away didn't cool me off as much as I had hoped it would, and as soon as I walked through the office doors, I found myself just as fired up as when I left. Perhaps it was beer-induced, but I decided my best course of action was to storm into his office, shut the door behind me, and shout, "WHAT IS YOUR PROBLEM?!?!" And I'm so glad I did because, in that moment, the way he looked at me told me that his outburst had absolutely nothing to do with me. He had been getting it from all sides, including the narcissist CEO, and I just happened to be the person in his line of fire when he couldn't take it anymore. For the first time, I felt like I saw him. We weren't so different after all—both of us were experiencing the same thing in the organization. We both felt stressed out, unappreciated, undervalued, and underutilized, and were questioning what we were doing in an organization that was clearly never going to change.

In this conversation, we made a human connection. There was no pretext, no agenda, no asks. We listened to each other, and probably heard each other for the first time since I'd started working there. We were vulnerable. There may have been tears and a hug. And for the rest of my time there (which wasn't terribly long because it was still a horrible place to work!), we were work BFFs and a bit of a support system in the midst of all the nonsense. It lightened the load a great deal.

Your shortcut to building relationships at work also happens to be one of the hardest things to do: Be vulnerable. Let people see the authentic you instead of the pretense you think you need to be successful. Open up and express what's really going on. Show your glorious flaws, and accept theirs as part of the package. There is not a single perfect person in the world and no one expects you to be the first.

For most people, this is an incredibly nerve-racking prospect. It's the last thing we're taught to do at work! You're supposed to put on the "professional" pretense at all costs, even though every single person you work with knows that's not real. It's not authentic. It's the dirty little secret that everyone knows but no one talks about, and that's what makes vulnerability the ultimate shortcut. Every person you work with is dying, on some level, to let their guard down. When you're vulnerable with others, you give them permission to be vulnerable with you. That's when you really get to the good stuff because that's when they're going to let you know what's actually going on—what they're thinking, feeling, aspiring to, and what they're really afraid of. That's when you connect and when the strongest relationships are formed.

LISTEN

You see it all the time in organizations—meetings that no one understands the point of because no real decisions ever get made. It's just half a dozen of the same people (or more!) talking, many times making the same points they've made over and over again in previous meetings but that were never acted upon. Still, they get up and beat their chest again and again and again in hopes that someday, someone will hear them!

And that's the problem. They're so desperate to be heard and to have their ideas validated that they don't stop to listen to what other people are saying. They are simply waiting to talk, going over in their head exactly what they want to say to make sure their point is clear, concise, and powerful. They aren't present with the people in the room, fully taking in what they have to say, considering the perspectives they're coming from, and considering ways to help them meet their goals. And that's the tragedy of the whole situation, because if they were fully present, they probably would have heard people expressing the same pain points, people who would make perfect allies!

Listening sounds like such as easy thing. Almost too easy, right? Don't confuse being in the same room when someone is talking with being present and really hearing what they have to say. In my coaching practice, I'm continually amazed at how many people I talk to every single week who feel like I'm the only person in their professional experience who actually listens to them.

So what does real listening look like?

- When you're listening, you're fully present with the person speaking. You're looking them in the eye, not typing notes into your computer.
- When you're listening, your body language is open. You do not have your arms crossed in front of you.
- When you're listening, you're trying to see things from that person's point of view, regardless of whether or not you agree with where they are coming from. Agreement is not the goal. Understanding and empathy are the goals.
- When you're listening, you're assuming the person who is speaking has positive intent with their message. You can hear and process what they're saying without cynicism.
- When you're listening, you're looking between the lines for what they're not saying, just as much as you're receiving what they are saying.
- When you're listening, you're not pushing back, debating, telling them why they're wrong, or making a case for what you want to do instead.

None of this is easy, but it's that last one that really messes people up. It might go without saying that when you're listening, you're not talking . . . but I find that keeping their mouth shut is one of the things that people struggle with the most. As one executive I coached said, "My biggest challenge is not challenging."

Constructive debate and exploring diverse viewpoints are critical to pulling the best work together. However, there is a distinct difference between debates that arise from that genuinely good goal, and ones in which people are seeking to be the winner of a pissing contest. One is driven by a genuine desire to learn, connect, and find compromise. The goal of the other is simply to be "right" and to feel validated for your beliefs. The former supports creating amazing relationships with your colleagues—the latter does not.

STOP EMAILING

I grew up in a small town in central Vermont. When I say small, I don't mean suburb—I mean there were fewer than fifty kids in my class when I graduated from high school. So when AOL start sending out those CDs in the mail, I begged my parents to sign up for it. (For those of you who don't remember this, in the old days AOL was the way most people got introduced to the internet.) Finally, after many months, they did, and I was one of the first kids in my neighborhood to get dial-up internet service at my house circa 1996-ish (at the lightening speed of 28.8 bps). Suddenly, a whole new world was available that took me beyond the confines of my small, boring, rural life. I was almost instantly addicted to the chat room and instant messaging (or IMing, as the kids called it), getting to know people from all over the world who had very different experiences than I did. They became my friends, accepting me in a way that the people I went to school with or my family did not. I genuinely cared about them and they cared for me in return. When it came to relationships, that was the most effective tool I had access to at the time.

Here's the thing: What works for a sixteen-year-old, shy, introverted girl does not work for professionals in the workplace. The digital tools we are all blessed with today give us the ability to communicate information easily through the touch of a button, but they also remove humanity from the process. Things like email, Slack, texting—they are great for so many things at work. Sharing a quick piece of information, passing a file back and forth, and scheduling meetings are all wonderful examples. However, these tools are horrible for anything that could be considered a human interaction. And that's exactly why people use them when they shouldn't—they're trying to avoid infusing humanity into the conversation because sometimes it's a really uncomfortable thing to do. But for our purposes here, it simply doesn't work.

If you want to build relationships with people, you've got to start treating them like real human beings. That means you have got to stop relying on email for your communication, and instead get up, walk over to their desk, and speak to them in person. And if you're in different geographic locations, use video chat liberally. When we can't hear people's voices or see their facial expressions, we lose information about how to read their intentions, and they aren't given the opportunity to experience the full breadth of our reactions. How many interpersonal squabbles could have been avoided if not for a misunderstood email?

CREATE WIN-WINS

When you started building your relationships strategically, you came up with a list of people who were moving in the same direction as you. Those relationships are the easier ones because you fundamentally want the same things and can help one another get there. Once you've got those relationships locked down, you want to look at those running in a different direction—those coworkers who want the same resources that you do but will use them to do diametrically opposed things. These are your workplace "enemies." Whether you like them or not is not the point—these are the people who consistently oppose what you're trying to achieve. The ones who are always speaking up in meetings and proposing a different tactic, or enumerating all the reasons why your plan won't work. They're the ones who are constantly getting in your way, and are probably the ones you're complaining about to your partner when you go home at night.

When you're working with people like this, your gut reaction is probably to fight them—to push back against them and tell them all the reasons why they're wrong. And that is exactly the wrong thing to do because that just exacerbates your differences, setting up a "you versus them" reality. Think about what happens when two groups of people are at war—the first thing they do is dehumanize each other. That makes it easy for them to fight. You're responsible for the reality that you're creating every single day—do you want to create a reality in which you're fighting, or do you want to create one that isn't adding that unnecessary stress?

If you've selected the latter option, your only choice is to diffuse the tension caused by differences between you to end the war. One of the most "zen" concepts in the world is to be like water. What does water do? It doesn't flow aggressively uphill. Instead, it flows downhill through every crack and crevice. When people say "go with the flow," this is what they mean—don't fight. Look for ways to align yourself with the direction other people are going.

So what does that mean for your workplace enemies? In *The Art of War*, Sun Tzu offers this advice: "Build your enemy a golden bridge to retreat across." What does he mean by that? He means that you have to make the idea of surrender more appealing than continuing the conflict. You know who your work enemies are. You know what resources they're fighting you to get. Now this is the hard part—you have to find a way to give it to them.

"But if their goal is different from mine, why would I give them what they want?!"

Remember that the goal you're working toward in this scenario is trying to build a relationship with this person. If you keep being the person denying them what they want, they're going to continue to paint you as the enemy, and that means they're going to keep fighting you. Instead, you need to throw them a bone—that's what disarms them and opens the door to a genuine relationship.

And here's the thing: You don't give them 100 percent of what they want. Find a way to give them part of what they want while allowing them to give you part of what you want. Another word for this is *compromise*—giving a little to get a little and creating a win-win scenario for you both. Remember, humans make decisions emotionally. That means your work relationship with this person depends on how they feel about you, not on logic. For that reason, it is better every single day of the week to get 50 percent, or 60 percent, or 70 percent of what you want and to give someone else a win, than it is to get 100 percent of what you want and piss someone else off—because when you piss someone off, that cuts your legs out from under you in all future projects involving that person. Compromising a little bit serves the experience you're trying to create, even if you have to give up a little. Do it consistently with a work enemy and you'll find they'll quickly become an ally because they know that when they work with you, they'll get a win. With a new ally on your side, you'll be able to make up any lost ground that the compromise cost you.

IT ALL MAKES LIFE EASIER

Think of an environment you genuinely enjoy coming into every day. One where you have the resources and support you need to achieve your goals, where you genuinely enjoy the people you work with, and where you feel appreciated for what you bring to the table. This is the value that creating great relationships offers. Show me someone who says, "I'm not here to make friends, I'm here to work," and I'll show you someone who probably isn't very happy in their professional experience. Yes, relationships take work and require compromise, but the payoff you'll get in return is huge.

CHAPTER 8

Find Your Beginner's Mind

In the beginner's mind, there are many possibilities. In the expert's mind, there are few.

—**Shunryu Suzuki**

GOAL FOR THIS CHAPTER:

Unchain yourself from your past experiences so you can look at each opportunity in front of you with a fresh set of eyes.

---

was once coaching a young professional who was only twenty-five years old and yet he was already feeling disillusioned with his work so early in his career. Conceptually, he could see that he had a good job at a company at which he enjoyed working and was doing work that he considered to be much more interesting and engaging than what his friends at different organizations were doing. But still, something was missing. Then, one day, his office hired a young professional just out of college. She was in a position that was similar to his, and so training and onboarding her became one of his "other duties as assigned." And this was the best thing that could have happened to him. He described to me how she approached everything they worked on with such wonder and youthful enthusiasm that it reminded him of what he loved about his job in the first place. Even though they were just a few years apart in age and experience, the pressure to meet deadlines, please everyone around him, and make quick decisions were enough to wear away at the excitement he had once brought to the job. His new colleague's influence helped him to find his beginner's mind again—he was able to look at situations through her eyes and see them for the opportunity they presented, rather than focusing on all the things that could go wrong.

OPEN YOUR MIND

In his popular TED Talk "Do Schools Kill Creativity"?"—and in a lesser-known talk he gave to the Royal Society for the Encouragement of Arts, Manufactures and Commerce (RSA) called "Changing Education Paradigms"—Sir Ken Robinson absolutely skewers the education system for the extent to which it undermines creativity by educating the population out of it. He argues that the standardization required by schools inhibits our ability for divergent thinking—the capacity to see lots of possible answers or interpretations for a single question. In the talk to the RSA, he noted a study from the book *Breakpoint and Beyond: Mastering the Future Today* in which researchers asked a group of fifteen hundred five-year-olds how they might use an everyday item, like a paper clip. Most people will be able to rattle off ten to fifteen answers to this question, but those who can engage in divergent thinking at higher levels will be able to come up with closer to two hundred answers because they don't allow rules and constraints to hold them back. For instance, they might question if they have to think of a paper clip as a small, metal object . . . or can they envision an object in paper-clip form that is five feet tall and made from rubber? When they administered this test to the children, 98 percent of them were able to engage in divergent thinking at the highest level. The researchers then followed those children and gave them the same test five years later— only 32 percent of them performed at the highest level. They administered the test again at fifteen years old—only 10 percent of them reached the highest level. And by the time they were adults, the percentage of the population who could utilize divergent thinking at the highest level dwindled to 2 percent. Robinson attributes this drop to the educational system, an environment that teaches us that there is only one right answer to a question. When students veer out of the accepted norms, the best thing that usually happens is that they are told they are wrong, which disincentivizes future outside-the-box thinking. The worst is they are put on medication for ADHD, effectively numbing them through the education process instead of allowing them to explore the unique genius they bring to the table.

By the time you make it to a professional environment as an adult, you're pretty well trained to look for the "right" answer, with the perception that there are consequences for not strictly adhering to the way things "should" be done. Do something a certain way for a while and you gain comfort in that experience, and become fearful that pushing outside of that comfort will lead to failure. You forget that what you were programmed to believe about failure in the twelve, sixteen, or twenty-plus years of schooling you had before you entered the workforce is not the same thing as failure *in* the workforce, when you're no longer chained to standardized test scores in subjects that may or may not contribute to your professional success. Fail an assignment in school and it goes on your permanent record (or so they threaten), but when you "fail" in the real world, you almost always have another opportunity to try again, learning from the first effort to inform the next attempt.

Eventually, if you do your job long enough, you hit expert level. You may even consider yourself a thought leader or a guru in your space, with people looking to you to know what the "right" answer is. And though experience can be a wonderful thing, it can also limit your perception of the possibilities because you're no longer exercising the mental muscles that allow you to actively engage in divergent thinking.

SELF-MASTERY EXERCISE

Test your ability to look at things differently. Think of a problem you're currently tackling at work—a project, a person, whatever. Use your journal to brainstorm as many solutions to this problem as you can possibly think of. Don't put any restrictions on yourself. You could even include "if/then" statements, like "If I had this budget, then I could achieve X," or "If I had three more full-time staff members supporting this project, then I could do Y."

When you're all out of ideas, count up your answers. Remember, the average person can discover about ten to fifteen. Where does your score fall?

No matter your answer, don't judge yourself. This is just to give you an idea of your jumping-off point. It's not an indicator of what you can achieve when you start working the necessary muscles. And if you're part of the lucky 2 percent that can do this really well, don't rest on your laurels. Make expansive thinking a conscious, active part of your day.

Embracing a beginner's mind will open you up to the world of possibilities that you have before you to support your goals and the experience you want to create.

The idea of a beginner's mind, or shoshin, comes from the world of Zen Buddhism and embraces an attitude of openness and genuine enthusiasm, clearing your mind of as many preconceived notions as possible. Sometimes the biggest thing that stands in the way of solving a problem is everything you think you know about it. The experience you've gathered over your professional career has also built up invisible walls around you, because once you get used to doing things a certain way—and become the expert in doing so—it's very difficult to see that options you've never tried before could work just as well. When you become really adept at using a hammer to solve problems, suddenly everything looks like a nail.

Think back to your first day as a professional, when everything was new. You hadn't learned the right or wrong ways to do things yet. You asked questions with genuine curiosity. Everyone you met was a source of knowledge and experience you could pull from, and you hadn't been sucked into the office gossip to tell you who you should and should not listen to yet. You approached every task, even if it was minor, with enthusiasm and excitement. This is the mindset you need to get back to.

Make no mistake, it's going to be uncomfortable at first. You're asking your mind to embrace change, and to sacrifice all the things you "know" in favor of considering things outside of your comfort zone. Remember that a beginner's mind is your natural state—it's what existed before school and life taught you all the things you "should" do. You're not creating something that was never there.

You're simply returning to something that has always been but just got a bit lost along the way.

CLEAR YOUR HEAD

Clearing your head of mental chatter is critical when you want to embrace a beginner's mind. The easiest way to do that is to focus on your breath, just for a moment. Think of this as a mini-meditation that you can do anywhere, anytime to allow yourself to open up to what's right in front of you. It's also a great thing to do when you're stressed out, anxious, angry, or experiencing anything negative that is not conducive to supporting the experience you want to create.

Here's how it works:

- Sit in a position where your back is straight and your feet are flat on the floor. Do not cross your arms or legs.
- Start inhaling slowly and deeply through your nose, so that you can feel the air passing down your throat, through your lungs, and all the way into your belly.
- Hold the breath in for a moment.
- Release the breath slowly through the mouth.

Throughout the exercise, keep your mind focused on the breath. Do it three to five times and you'll find yourself almost instantly more present and focused. This simple act has calmed down your whole nervous system and reduced your stress, allowing you to better access the parts of the brain that allow you to see things differently.

SELF-MASTERY EXERCISE

Revisit the list of ways you brainstormed to solve the problem you wanted to tackle from the previous exercise, but this time do your deep breathing for one minute. Then look at the last list you created and see if you can discover any more options to tackle the problem that hadn't occurred to you before.

LET THE PAST GO

I'm sure you can already think of a ton of ways to utilize a beginner's mind in your daily life, but one of the most often overlooked is in your relationships with your coworkers. Oftentimes, it's those relationships that enable (or prevent) you from fully exploring the range of tactical options available. It's not that you don't see the possibilities—it's that you rule them out completely because the obstacle you have to hop over is dealing with people you work with. Fix the relationship with your coworkers, and that instantly opens up new strategic possibilities.

Embracing a beginner's mindset is all about existing in the present moment and not allowing the past to inform the actions you're taking right now. The present moment is the only moment that matters. The past is gone. No matter what's happened, you can't do anything to change it—the best you can do is change your thoughts about it or just let it go entirely. If your history with a person does not serve your current goals, you have an obligation to yourself not to let it impact you. This is not about letting the other person off the hook—this is about advancing the experience you are trying to create for yourself. In every moment, you have a chance for a new beginning and a fresh outlook.

Some people go in the opposite direction—they live for the future and everything that could take place with the people in question. I hate to point out the obvious, but the future hasn't happened yet! You can't say for sure how things will turn out, what people around you will say or do, or if that person you don't like today will turn out to be your most staunch ally tomorrow. If you don't give them a chance, you never allow that future to materialize. You're cutting off the possibility based on things that have happened already . . . which you can't go back and change!

When you live in the present moment, you let the past go and give the future a chance to unfold in a way that serves the professional experience you want, rather than reinforcing what you currently have today. Though we're talking about it in the context of working well with others, you're also doing this for your own good. You're allowing yourself the opportunity to open more doors and achieve more success than would be possible if you were just working on an island by yourself.

CULTIVATE YOUR OWN PSYCHOLOGICAL SAFETY

Between 2013 and 2015, Google conducted an extensive study to try to understand what the critical attributes of a successful team were. They assumed they would find that the ideal team was made up of people with specific personality traits and skill sets. Instead, what they found was that the most important factor in creating a high-performance team was not who was on it, but rather, how they felt about one another. Far and away, the biggest contributing factor to a successful team at Google was that team members felt a high degree of psychological safety with one another—they felt safe to take risks and be vulnerable. Not only were the people on those teams less likely to leave Google, but they were more likely to harness the power of diverse ideas from their teammates. As a result, the projects they worked on brought in more money, and they were more likely to be rated as effective by executives. All of this was achieved simply because of how they felt about one another.

We touched on the importance of vulnerability in the previous chapter, but vulnerability also plays an integral role in cultivating a beginner's mindset. You've got to feel safe asking the "dumb" questions. That's what a beginner's mind requires—exploring every option as though it were your first day at work. You want to be curious; to consider tactics that you dismissed years ago that may be just the answer you're looking for today; and to explore your past failures to see what you can draw from them to create future success. Modern organizations can sometimes pressure you into acting like you know it all. When you're trying to cultivate an image of being "the expert," all of these things become very difficult to do. However, when you embrace being a beginner, all those "dumb" questions become very important.

Still, if those questions aren't expressed outwardly to others, they don't help anyone. When you're on a team that lacks psychological safety, there are a lot of good reasons to hold back questions—if you're working with someone who has thrown you under the bus in the past, you don't want to look dumb in front of them or give them a reason to ridicule you in front of others. Practicing ignorance to embrace the beginner's mind takes very real courage and humility, but doing so allows you to bring other members of your team on your journey with you. Sure, you will always have the cynics, and there's nothing much you can do about that. But what if you could help other members of your team explore options in a way they wouldn't have thought of before, simply by asking the "dumb" questions? When that happens, you're not only serving your personal goals—you're also serving the group and elevating everyone in it.

You must understand that psychological safety starts with you and the story you're telling yourself about the people you're working with. I was once coaching someone who was having constant interpersonal problems with someone she worked with, and their inability to communicate was bleeding into their respective teams' desire to work with each other. Every week we would peel back the layers of issues the two had, trying to solve each problem so communication could improve. One week, we hit on one I had never experienced before—she felt that he approached work like a reality TV show because he had been on a fairly high-profile reality competition show years before. And that's when I said something I never anticipated having to say in my coaching career: "You cannot hold against someone what they did on a reality TV show seven years ago!" In this case, my client was letting a story that was not only out of context, but also very out-of-date impact the relationship she was having with this person in the present time.

What if you could simply remove all those past stories that don't serve your work or your team today? The answer is that you can . . . if you make the decision to do so.

ALWAYS ASSUME POSITIVE INTENT

To fully embrace and express a beginner's mind, you have to feel psychologically safe. It's not possible to do so if the story you're playing over and over again in your head is that your coworkers are out to get you. Therefore, the easiest way to start changing the story you have about the people you're working with is simply to assume that, no matter what, they have positive intent.

The fact is most people do not come into work every day with the aim of causing problems or sabotaging their colleagues. Most people are coming in with the genuine goal of trying to do a good job. If they are raising issues and concerns, it's probably not a personal attack—they're doing it because they are trying to serve the goals as they understand them. Might their tactics be misguided? Do they go against their coworkers in the process? Yes. But the logic is usually not "I'm going to really stick it to Johnny Jones in marketing." They are trying to do their job in the best way they know how.

I say "most people" because, unfortunately, there are people who make work a personal vendetta. These are the people who see their only path to success as walking on the backs of others, and their actions are so impactful that we sometimes forget that the things that motivate them are not the motivators for the majority of the population. But for the moment, let's put those people to the side. They are the minority, and we're going to explore how to handle them a few chapters from now.

So, given that most of your coworkers have positive intent, you simply need to change the story you're telling yourself. Remember what you learned about projection back in chapter 4—what you see others doing is nothing more than a reflection of things going on in your own head: insecurities, fears, feelings of not being good enough, memories of past experiences that were painful. If you've had a negative feeling about someone in the past, you're going to create a story that perpetuates that feeling into the future. Instead, you can choose to be aware of what's going on and force yourself to create a different story in regards to your situation by telling yourself that the opposite of whatever you're feeling is true—that will change the way you act and feel about the person. Here's the trick:

> It's not what I think of myself.
> It's not what they think of me.
> It's what I think they think of me.

I learned this from a friend of mine who would go into the same Starbucks every morning to get his cup of coffee and would have the same barista waiting on him every day. He didn't think she liked him, and having to interact with her first thing in the morning started his day off on the wrong foot. So he used this trick, and before going in to get his cup of coffee, he simply told himself that she didn't hate him. In fact, she totally wanted him (yes, he thinks a lot of himself). And based on this, he behaved completely differently toward her, which, over time, made her behave completely differently toward him. He solved the problem by creating a different story, believing it, and acting as if it were true.

Now, you probably don't want to tell yourself that the people you work with totally want you (that's an HR problem waiting to happen!), but you can use this trick in other ways. For example, if you're working with a group of people and don't think they respect you, be aware that it's probably more a reflection of your own self-doubt than it is an accurate picture of their perception of you.

You've arrived at the root of the problem—now just change the story. Act as though it's your first day of work and tell yourself that they think you're amazing at what you do and that you'll be able to get them onboard with your plan, even if they have some questions and concerns that you'll need to account for (because that's life in the professional world!). Visualize that in your head and think about how it would make you feel to have that be true. Then, just behave accordingly. When you go into your next conversation with them, act as if that reality were true—you'll behave much differently than if you think they don't respect you, and you can expect a more positive result from it.

You might read this and think, "You just made that up! It's not real! How can that possibly work?" Here's the thing: It's made up either way. You don't know what will happen because you can't predict the future. The best thing you can do is set yourself up for what will serve the experience you're trying to create. Remember, beginners don't feel stress and anxiety when they walk into their first meeting at their first job because no one has taught them that they should. They feel excited, like they finally have a seat at the table.

SELF-MASTERY EXERCISE

Think of someone you work with who you think doesn't like you. They're the one who is always shooting down your ideas, pushing back in meetings, making unrealistic requests, etc. Take out your journal and write the story you're telling yourself about this person.

Then read it over and consider whether that story supports your having a positive working relationship with this person. If it doesn't, rewrite the story. What type of relationship do you need to have with this person to create a positive professional experience for yourself? How can this person help you meet your goals? How do you want this person to perceive you?

Finally, ask yourself this: If my revamped story were true, and I had never learned that I wasn't supposed to like them, then how would I behave toward this person? How would I speak to them? Act around them? How would I include them in my projects? Would I go out to coffee/lunch/drinks with them?

Try behaving as if that second story were true for a little bit and see where it gets you.

HAVE FUN!

I was once stuck in an email chain back-and-forth with a person on the academic support team at my college because I was trying to figure out what I needed to do to get approval for something and I had been told two different stories by members of the administration. We had reached the point where I didn't particularly care what the answer to the question was—I just wanted to know the information I was receiving was correct. After the fourth round of email with this support person, I finally embraced my beginner's mind and asked the dumb question: "I understand you don't have the answer to this question. Can we just email this other person and ask them to look it up?" Almost instantly, I received a long-winded message back from her boss that CC'ed several other people telling me that I was unprofessional and uncollegiate for having the gall to tell her to email another person. The very first thing I thought (apart from the fact that I still didn't get an answer to my question) was "My God . . . what a miserable person this guy is."

It's people like this who have made me hate the term *professional*. Sure, I use it in this book to describe the experience you're trying to create because it's the word that many working people identify with. But if I'm honest, the thought of being a "professional" makes me cringe in some respects. It's not that I think there's anything wrong with being or acting like a professional, conceptually. It's just that I think it's a code word that people use when they want to encourage generally stuffy behavior that lacks all personality. Why would you want to create an experience that requires you to go into work every day and act like you have a giant stick up your ass? That doesn't sound ideal at all!

One of the best things about embracing a beginner's mind is that it allows you to explore the feeling of joy, wonder, and playfulness that you had when you were a kid, before anyone taught you that life was supposed to be serious. Think about how a kid approaches life: They explore. They're curious. They love unconditionally. They're wonderfully authentic.

How would your work experience change if you could approach every day, every project, every task, with that same sense of childlike joy? What if you could transport yourself back to that time when you hadn't learned how to expect the worst yet? You may not be able to travel back in time, but you can bring that sensibility to your current work experience. Give it a try. Next time you find yourself dreading a task, take a moment, do your breathing, and ask yourself how you would have approached it before you learned to hate it. Tell yourself that you'll find a way to make a game of it, even if it's by giving yourself a simple reward like a candy when you're done. Be playful. Make it fun. See how that changes your experience.

CHAPTER 9

Boost Your Confidence

The most common way people give up their power is by thinking they don't have any.

—Alice Walker

GOAL FOR THIS CHAPTER:

Effectively express confidence in your ideas in a way that gets others just as excited about them as you are.

Almost every executive I have ever coached has told me some version of the following dirty little secret: When new ideas are presented to them, they push back no matter what to see how confident the person who's presenting them is. The executive might love the idea, but if the person championing it doesn't defend it when it's challenged, that's an indication they won't be able to see it through execution. Why should the executive have confidence in them if they don't have confidence in themselves? But if the person stands their ground and keeps championing the idea in the face of adversity, it gives the executive confidence that they are the person for the job.

How many good ideas have been presented that never made their way to reality simply because the person presenting them didn't do it with confidence? It's easy to think of confidence as something you need for yourself, but confidence at work is just as much about helping other people to see opportunities and feel amazing about pursuing them. When you present confidently, you help other people feel comfortable—with you, with the idea, and with contributing their time and energy to it.

MOST PEOPLE ARE NOT CONFIDENT AT WORK

If you have issues around confidence at work, consider yourself in good company. If you look at the numbers, anywhere between 60 to 80 percent of people report that they lack confidence at work . . . and that number tends to be about 10 percent higher if you're a woman. Some of those are people whom you would never expect— leaders and executives in your organization whom you might look at and think are the epitome of confidence. When no one is listening, they will admit that they still have that little voice in the back of their heads telling them their idea won't work or that they're not good enough . . . They've just learned how to quiet it down and project the right tone and demeanor to the people they are leading because they know that's what the team needs from them. That motivation gives them the ability to push past any discomfort they have to take care of the team. Expressing confidence is about being of service to people. If you're nervous, they will be nervous. If you're apprehensive, they will be apprehensive. If you're uncomfortable, they will be uncomfortable. But if you believe in yourself and what you're presenting, then the chance of them returning the sentiment skyrockets.

Some people conflate a lack of confidence with being introverted. Let's be clear: The two are not related. Introversion and extroversion is about where you get your energy. Introverts recharge by being on their own, curling up on the couch to veg on Netflix or read a good book, or by spending time with their partner or a few close friends. Extroverts, on the other hand, get their energy from other people—they love being out in a crowd, at a party or networking event, mingling and making small talk. But that doesn't mean that extroverts have a confidence gene that introverts were born without. If that were true, every successful CEO or public figure would be an extrovert, and we know that's not the case. Bill Gates, Warren Buffett, Mark Zuckerberg, and Barack Obama are all examples of highly successful people who would classify themselves as introverts. In other words, introversion isn't the problem—it just happens to be a convenient excuse. "I'm an introvert . . . I can't do that." Well, sure you can . . . if you make the decision to do it.

In many cases, shyness contributes more to the problem of not expressing confidence than introversion does. Shyness may seem to overlap with introversion, but it is separate and distinct. Introversion is about whether or not you are motivated to be around large groups of people. Shyness is feeling uncomfortable or inhibited when you interact with others because you're overestimating the likelihood of them perceiving you negatively. Just because you're an introvert doesn't mean you are shy—you may be perfectly fine interacting with others. You'll just need a break or a nap afterward to recharge.

Remember, people make decisions emotionally and justify them rationally, and one of the easiest ways to get people to go along with our ideas is to be likable. So let's think about the qualities we might identify with someone who is inherently unlikable or unfriendly:

- They seem standoffish, judgmental, and unapproachable. They have closed body language, and only talk to people they know.
- They talk about themselves a lot, and perhaps bring an air of superiority to the discussion.
- They don't make eye contact when you're having a conversation with them and seem totally disinterested in getting to know you.

That doesn't seem like the type of person I would like to be around or whose team I want to be on at work! Well, guess what—people who are shy do the exact same things. Of course, they are not doing it with the intention of being unfriendly or unlikable. Quite the opposite, actually. They are worried the people they are struggling to interact with aren't going to like them! We've explored how the stories you play in your head dictate how you behave and what you experience. When people are shy, here's the story they're playing in their heads when they're around groups: "They're judging me . . . I don't want to say the wrong thing . . . What if they think I'm stupid?" Remember that we subconsciously feel what we're seeing in other people. When you're planning for the worst possible thing to happen, you're eliciting a negative perception from others in return.

CONFIDENCE IS FOR OTHER PEOPLE

If shyness is what is holding you back from expressing confidence at work, you need to remember that confidence is not for you. It's for the people you're working with. Take another look at the story that shy people are playing in their head in the previous paragraph. What do those statements have in common? They are all about you, how you feel, and what you're afraid of. There is not a moment's attention given to what the people around you need from you.

The number one reason that things fail in organizations—everything from small projects to large initiatives—is because the people in charge of spearheading those projects fail to gain alignment from others and bring them along. In order to do that effectively, you need to help other people feel comfortable—comfortable with you and with the work they're doing; they need to have the sense that things are under control. That's what happens when you express confidence outwardly. Think of it as a part of doing your job well and meeting your goals, because when you help other people, you inherently help yourself.

SELF-MASTERY EXERCISE

When it comes to psychology, you can find evidence to support almost any perspective. There are researchers and academics who argue that being shy is partly genetic—that there are biological and sociability traits that you're born with that simply can't be changed. While there may be some truth to that, I'm of the camp that believes that shyness can be overcome if you have the motivation and make the decision to do the work that decision requires.

If shyness is something you think might be inhibiting your ability to be confident, think of a situation you have coming up—like

presenting your ideas to others or making the case for something you
would like to do—and apply these tactics to it.

- **See yourself in a role.** Sometimes it can help to envision yourself as an actor on a stage. You're not you when you're standing up
  in front of your audience—you're the person they need you to be.
  What would that person say? What would they do? What type of
  language would they use? How would they inspire the people in
  front of them?
- **Assume it will go well.** Shyness gets in your way because you're
  telling yourself an ugly story in your head about what might occur.
  Don't be so hard on yourself. Think about what it would be like to
  walk into the room with the conviction that the people in it will be
  open and receptive to what you have to say, and that you're serving the team with your ideas.
- **Ask questions.** When shyness takes over, it can be easy to default to talking about the thing you know best—yourself! Instead,
  turn the focus on the audience. Who are they? What do they care
  about? What are their goals? Sometimes a simple question can
  take the pressure off you to be the only one driving the conversation. Be careful to ask the question out of genuine curiosity, and
  then sit back and take in their answer completely.

Take out your journal and write about how you might apply these
strategies to your specific situation. This will help you visualize what
achieving success looks like before you even walk through your office door.

CONFIDENCE IS A SKILL

It's easy to approach the subject of confidence with the perspective
that some people are born with it and some people are not, but the
reality is that confidence is a skill that everyone needs to spend
some energy developing. Some people are blessed to start their careers with a work style that naturally exudes confidence. Others

bring different attributes to the table that are important but aren't as strong at the confidence game, or they may have had their confidence beaten down by horrible bosses who made them feel like nothing they did was good enough. No matter where you start, anyone can learn to exude confidence. The more you practice, the more confidence you'll development.

SELF-MASTERY EXERCISE

Who's your confidence role model? Think of someone you work with who is your very definition of confident. Ask yourself what they're doing to make you think that. Brainstorm in your journal. How do they carry themselves? What do they say? How do they interact with others? What do they do when people push back on their ideas?

Once you have a good list going, simply start to mirror those attributes. This is your opportunity to practice what confidence looks like. Keep track of the things you try, and the reactions you get from your coworkers to get a sense of what works and what doesn't. Remember, this is a work in progress. If it doesn't feel uncomfortable, you're probably not pushing yourself hard enough.

Looking for more inspiration, or can't think of a great role model to follow? Take a look back at chapter 3 and, for lack of a better term, act like a D. The dominant work style is what people typically envision when they think of a natural leader—the ones who seem to exude confidence without even trying. Imagine what a person with that style would do and then practice doing the same thing.

START BEFORE YOU LEAVE THE HOUSE

In 2014, Naval Admiral William H. McRaven gave a commencement speech at the University of Texas, where he told the graduates that if you want to change the world, you have to start by making your bed. His argument was that the little things in life matter. If you can't do the little things right, you can't do the big things right.

In many respects, it's the same way with confidence. When you leave the house in the morning, make sure you feel amazing. When someone feels great, they can't help but exude confidence to the people around them. Do whatever you need to do to get there—make a great breakfast, get a workout in, play power music as you're getting ready, or take a minute to remind yourself of everything you've got going for you. Even putting on a great outfit can change the way you see yourself, and thus change the way you see the world. And remember that if you don't have confidence in yourself, you can't expect anyone to have confidence in you—look in the mirror before you leave, strike a power pose, and tell yourself that you're going to knock them dead at work because everyone there thinks you're smart and amazing at your job. Remember, you are in complete control of everything you say and do when you're in your own environment. That means there's no excuse for not leaving the house feeling your very best.

WATCH YOUR BODY LANGUAGE

I was an incredibly shy, awkward kid in school, and I remember that my younger brother used to make fun of me because I would walk through the halls of school with my head down and my shoulders hunched. I was expressing my lack of confidence to everyone who saw me, and I didn't need to say a word to do it.

Expressing confidence starts before you ever open your mouth. It impacts the way you see yourself, and it impacts what your coworkers think of you. What does your body language express? Are you sitting up straight, or are you bent over on your computer or your phone? Is your body constrained, with your arms crossed, or do you look open and relaxed? Are you smiling, or do you have a cross look on your face? Be very aware of the messages you're sending to people simply by how you're sitting at the meeting room table. If people think that you're angry or closed off to dialogue, they are not going to feel comfortable engaging with you.

BACK OTHER PEOPLE UP

Women who served in the White House under Barack Obama made it a point to help one another out. The men they worked with had a bad habit of glossing over their contributions in meetings, and then subsequently taking credit for their ideas, so the women started "amplifying" the contributions that each of them made by repeating it back to the room and crediting the original author. This made sure the men in the room couldn't ignore the idea or take credit for it later.

Regardless of your gender, one of the easiest things you can do to practice confidence is to support your coworkers. Think someone has a good idea in a meeting? Don't bite your tongue and wait for others to speak up—say it! Not only will you generate goodwill from the people you're supporting, but it will give you a chance to express your ideas in a safe context where risk is minimal. Saying "Great idea, Johnny" does not usually come with a long-term commitment.

EMBRACE BOLD IDEAS

Go big or go home! Seventy-six percent of people see boldness as an important attribute of an effective leader. Give the people what they want—inspiration! It's about providing a vision of a future state the team can achieve together that will elevate everyone. That's what gets people excited and makes them want to come on the journey with you.

A boss I once had constantly told us to put our stake in the ground—look at all the information available and make a call. Some people found this idea debilitating because they never felt completely confident in their ideas. Others found it empowering and exciting. To embrace bold ideas, you have to tell the story of it being an amazing opportunity, even if it leaves some uncertainty. Understand that in life, you'll rarely be 100 percent sure about anything, so don't hold yourself to that standard. Try to get to 70 percent and then put your stake in the ground. If you're 70 perent sure, there's not much more ground you can realistically gain.

When you're embracing bold ideas, it can be really helpful to surround yourself with people who believe in you. Lots of people will tell you all the things you won't be able to achieve. Remember, that's their story—you're under no obligation to embrace it and make it yours. Find the people who inspire you to see the world in new ways and go after the things you would have avoided because you didn't think they were achievable.

And don't get caught up in the execution! You can figure that out later, and the very fact that you have the courage to express big ideas in the first place will put you in a new category. So many people avoid bringing the bold ideas to the table because they're worried about all the things that could go wrong when they're trying to achieve them. Here's the thing: When leaders in organizations present a big, bold vision, they've rarely thought through all the steps to make it a reality. The vision provides the destination, and you utilize the collective mind power of your team to figure out the specific routes you'll take to get there.

KNOW YOUR TALKING POINTS

Whether you like politics or loathe it, there's a lot to learn about how to sell ideas from watching what the candidates do on the campaign trail. Being from New Hampshire, I get a front-row seat when all the would-be candidates for president show up in my backyard a full two years ahead of the general election to stake their claim in the nation's first primary. Regardless of party affiliation or their position on the issues, there are a few things they all do really well: They know their talking points, and they say them over and over and over again, even if they are not the answer to the question being asked!

When you're presenting your big ideas, be a politician (in the very best way!). Make sure you have your message down to a clear, concise set of talking points. You want to find the balance between giving away enough information that people understand what you want to do and why, while holding back the nitpicky details.

People who have confidence down to a science tend to speak in bullet points.

- I want to do X.
- This is why I want to do X.
- This is what I think the impact of X will be.

They don't go into long-winded explanations of each and every point, and it's that unapologetic focus that gives the impression they know exactly what they're talking about.

It sounds so simple, but this is what trips a lot of people up. They want to present all the additional validation for their ideas, but they lose their audience in the extra details. People are busy. They have a lot on their minds and are probably mentally multitasking as you're presenting. Share enough to give them a taste—this allows the broad idea to speak for itself in a way that people can easily receive the information. State your bullet points . . . and then pause. Silence can be unnerving, but the pause is critical! Just let it be for a moment. Not only does it articulate absolute confidence in your ideas, but it also allows the room time to consider the information. And then it gives people an opportunity to ask questions. Chances are, someone is going to break the silence and engage with you, even if it's to push back on the idea. This is a good thing! It opens a dialogue, which instantly takes your idea from a concept to something that is under consideration to become a tangible reality.

What happens if they don't ask questions? That's an opportunity as well. Turn it on the room and ask them if they have any questions so far. When you ask them, give them your full attention and use active listening to repeat their perspective back to them. For example: "So what I heard you say is that you like the idea but you think the timeline I'm proposing should be increased to accommodate this other project that's already under way. Do I have that right?" You're doing a number of things here:

- You're emphasizing that you heard them. In *Five Dysfunctions of a Team*, Patrick Lencioni beautifully points out that people don't need to have their own ideas implemented to buy into a

decision. They simply need to have their ideas heard, understood, and considered in the context of the decision.

- You're validating their perspective. You may not fully agree
with it, but you're not instantly challenging it either. This will
help to disarm them if they were planning a full-on attack, and
it opens the doors to creating a win-win scenario.

- You're giving them an opportunity to clarify their feedback.
Sometimes when people repeat things back to us, we hear it in
a new way. Now they have a chance to say "No, that's not quite
what I meant . . ." and offer additional information.

- You're making them feel taken care of, as if you have the situation under control and are seeking to collaborate and include
other perspectives. Always remember that how you make people feel matters far more than the specific words that come out
of your mouth.

And if the room still stays silent when you prompt them for
questions, use that as an opportunity to reinforce the idea. "So if
no one has any questions, that means that everyone is on board
with this as a concept?" Best-case scenario, everyone nods their
head yes in agreement. In that case, you've won the meeting. You
don't need to walk out with a fully fleshed-out plan. You just need
to walk out with agreement so you can get to work on next steps.
And worst-case scenario is that someone says no, and that's just
another chance to open that dialogue.

This process can be used whether you're presenting to a group
of people or one-on-one to a boss or colleague. Present your idea
clearly and allow them a moment to consider and engage. If they
don't ask questions or push back, close by reinforcing the validity
of the concept.

TAKE CONSTRUCTIVE FEEDBACK WELL

Inherent to some of the discussion in the previous point, it's critical that if your coworkers offer constructive criticism, you take it in stride. Confident people don't look for validation of their ideas externally, because they walk in knowing that it's a good idea. So when others push back, they don't need to enter into a long, drawn-out explanation of why their point of view misses the mark. It doesn't serve your goal to do so—it just derails you from your talking points and quickly puts you on the defensive.

If constructive feedback comes up, don't fight it. Embrace it. Use it as a chance to validate their perspective and make them feel heard by asking additional questions:

- I hadn't thought of that. Tell me more.
- Can you give me an example?
- How would you address this problem?

Know that when you solicit additional information, you're demonstrating through your actions that you're doing your due diligence. And in the process, you may uncover scenarios you hadn't initially considered, which will help you later.

When the dialogue concludes, make sure you thank the person for offering their perspective. Constructive criticism is rarely received well and almost instantly puts the receiver on the defensive. In accepting and even encouraging it, you're demonstrating confidence in your perspective.

And no matter what your coworkers say or do to push back on your ideas, resist the urge to go after them, either directly or by engaging in office gossip about them when you think no one is listening. In the short-term, it may feel great, but those things always come back to bite you later. Truly confident people don't need to walk over others or engage in personal attacks in order to have their voices heard. They let the ideas speak for themselves.

SELF-MASTERY EXERCISE

Consider the things you do or think when you start to lose confidence: Maybe you fidget, or your heart starts to pound, or you start rambling instead of staying on message. Take out your journal and write about what you experience so that you can be aware of your confidence triggers. When they pop up, stop, take a breath, and remind yourself that when you're bringing your confident self, you're doing what the people in the room need you to do. Then go back to the tactics in this chapter and apply the first one that comes to you to get yourself back on track.

NO DOESN'T MEAN NO FOREVER. IT MEANS NO FOR NOW.

Marketing professionals follow the rule of seven—the idea that a potential buyer has to hear a message at least seven times before they make the decision to buy from you. So you express your idea, you follow your talking points, you engage in a dialogue . . . and the ultimate decision still comes down against you. Pay it no mind. Ideas get shot down for any number of reasons that have nothing to do with the merit of the idea—there could be other initiatives coming down from the top that you don't know about, or the budget just got slashed, or the approved direction is about to change. Or maybe they just haven't heard the idea enough times to give it their full attention in the context of a hectic work schedule. Don't make the assumption that your idea isn't worthy. It just may not be it's time yet.

So many people give up after they're told no one time. If you truly have confidence in what you're putting out, you need to embrace your inner politician and look for opportunities to speak your ideas over and over and over again, knowing that it's okay to be a little annoying about it because that gives your message a chance to be heard. I once had a CEO tell me, "You've come to me with the same idea seven or eight times . . . now I know you're serious."

IT DOESN'T HAPPEN OVERNIGHT

Remember, confidence is not something you're going to go from zero to 100 percent on within a day. It took time to get to where you are today, and it will take time to get to where you want to be. As with any new skill, it takes practice, commitment, and consistency. Give it time and have faith that you will get out of it what you put into it. If you make small efforts every single day to boost your confidence and express it outwardly, it will add up. Just like making your bed in the morning, it's the little things you do every day that will lead to your success.

CHAPTER 10

Working with Enemies

In the practice of tolerance, one's enemy is the best teacher.
—His Holiness the fourteenth Dalai Lama

GOAL FOR THIS CHAPTER:

Don't let the naysayers get you down. Learn what motivates their behavior so you can put it in perspective.

A friend of mine once told me about an experience a friend of hers had when he met the Dalai Lama. He asked him about his perceptions of China, a country that has, for decades, decimated his homeland of Tibet and whose officials once referred to him as a "wolf in monk's clothing." He replied that it is easy to love your friends. But China is his special friend, one that gives him the opportunity to practice tolerance and love when it's difficult.

Work friends, work allies, work husbands/wives . . . these are the people you unconditionally trust and who add value, camaraderie, levity, and support to your day. But let's face it—you're never going to feel great about everyone you work with. People are going to put down your ideas, be constantly critical and negative, make you feel like an impostor, or hate you for no apparent reason. You still need to coexist with them in a way that maintains your perspective and allows you to create a work experience you love. Let's explore the fascinating world of work enemies.

Your work enemies aren't necessarily bad, evil people. But they're not the people who are going to help you meet your goals or get things done. If you're from the south, you might look at a work enemy and say, "Bless their heart." Here are some other telltale signs of a work enemy:

- They're naysayers (they'll call it being the devil's advocate) and never lack something critical to say about any project that is up for discussion.
- They bring a negative attitude with them to work every day, always looking at things with the worst possible perspective. If you see them in a good mood, it's so rare that you become suspicious of the reasons.
- They're the people who stand up in meetings to grandstand against anything that deviates from the way you've always done things before. They may raise their voice at anyone who questions them.
- They're competitive and see things as win/lose scenarios—if someone else is successful, they fail. It could be something small or large, anything from someone else getting a staff award over them to battles over budget or organizational resources.

In some cases, they might be downright oblivious to the impact they're having. In others, they are intentionally working against you. They could be your boss, your peer, or your subordinate—anyone in any position could be a work enemy.

In chapter 2, we looked at the difference between fault and responsibility—what other people do is not your fault, but how you react and what you contribute to the situation is your responsibility. This is never truer than with the people who drive you crazy at work. You must really internalize that they can only ruin your day if you allow them to—only you can give them that power over your experience.

PUT THEM IN PERSPECTIVE

The story you tell yourself is everything when it comes to dealing with the challenging people at work. When you don't like someone, or they're going against you, it may be easy to tell yourself, "They're a horrible person and impossible to work with—they just want to make everything difficult," but does that story serve you? Does it get you closer to your goals? Does it help you deal with this person effectively? Probably not. What if, instead, you told yourself, "This person is a challenge to deal with, but they're probably just trying to do the best they can."

Here's the thing to really understand about your work enemies: Most of them are not being intentionally challenging with their behavior. About 50 percent of the workforce brings a generally more skeptical attitude with them to the office. It's innate—it's simply much easier for them to see the negative in things than it is to see the positive. It may seem like they are doing everything they can to throw a wrench into things or bring down the mood of the room, but if you engage them in an honest chat, you'll find that they genuinely believe they're fighting the good fight, that they are trying to do their job and do right by the organization.

When you're dealing with a naysayer, most often it's a matter of a clash in work styles—you're either very different than they are, or you're very, very similar and you're butting heads. I find that the crux of the issue tends to be how people deal with conflict. People generally fall into one of two categories: Those who get revved up in the face of a conflict and might actively seek it out, and those who avoid conflict like the plague and want to jump under the table when it's happening. Those whom you might categorize as work enemies generally have a much higher tolerance for conflict than your average bear. They love a good debate, enjoy playing devil's advocate, and do not back down in the face of a challenge. It's fun for them, like a game. Pair them with someone who is very conflict avoidant, and they will overpower them and leave them feeling undervalued and unappreciated. Pair them with someone who is equally tolerant of conflict, and that's an ongoing interpersonal conflict waiting to happen because neither of them is going to back down. Rarely have I dealt with any major interpersonal issues at work that did not involve at least one person with a high tolerance for conflict.

HAVE EMPATHY

Let's take a moment to step into their shoes. Challenging people at work are not unaware that they're perceived as challenging. In fact, some of them may joke about it and outwardly hold it up as a point of pride. Don't be fooled—that's a coping mechanism. It's a way of them putting up a wall so that you never find out that they're probably not very happy. You've learned that the contributions you make every day add up to the experience you have in whatever context you're in. Whether intentional or not, when you can only see the negative qualities in people, ideas, and projects, that doesn't lead to a very happy experience. And when people are unhappy, they unconsciously want other people around them to be unhappy. Misery loves company.

SELF-MASTERY EXERCISE

Think about when you've been unhappy at work for an extended period of time. Try to think of an example from a previous job that doesn't involve the coworker who now gives you the most trouble. What did that past experience feel like for you?

Here's an example: Perhaps you didn't think anyone listened to your ideas. You kept putting them out there over and over again, but it felt like you were talking to a wall the whole time. You watched people around you achieve successes, thinking you were always playing second fiddle to someone else's victories. You felt unvalued and unappreciated, like no matter how much work or thought you put into an idea, no one "got it." You questioned what you were doing with your life, but managed to convince yourself that this was as good as it was going to get. And because you were unhappy at work, you took that feeling home with you. Maybe it impacted your relationships with your friends and family, to the point where you felt alone, like no one in your life understood.

Take whatever feelings this exercise conjured up and ask yourself how you would feel about the person you're having trouble with now if that was what was running through their head every day. Would you see them differently? Would it change your perspective?

GIVE THEM THEIR POWER BACK

They may act powerful, but often the naysayers of the world are experiencing a profound sense of powerlessness. Think about the example in the self-mastery exercise on the previous page—does that sound like the mindset of a powerful person? The modern workplace has a serious problem with empowerment, typically reserving it for those at the very top. That means that a good chunk of the workforce goes through decades of their career not feeling like they have much control over anything. Some studies report that as much as 79 percent of respondents have had or are currently experiencing micromanagement, with 85 percent reporting that being micromanaged negatively impacts their morale.

You may not be able to change the reality of the workplace or help fix the micromanagement problem, but you can give someone their power back in how you choose to work with them. When something causes us stress, our natural instinct is either to avoid it or fight it. Since you're aware of that fact, you can have the presence of mind to choose a third option: Embrace it. Take a lesson from the Dalai Lama and use this as an opportunity to practice tolerance and love with the most difficult people. Be the person who listens to them, asks about their point of view, and tries to find win-win compromises so that they can experience success.

In any interactions where they're playing their usual naysayer game, keep your cool and focus on how you can flow with the situation. Don't push back with any version of "You're wrong, I disagree with you, and here are all the facts I have on my side." That takes the focus off the end goal and puts it on the debate. Remember, people like this are usually a bit competitive—the minute there's a contest to be won, that's going to be their priority, work relationships be damned.

Here's one way this could play out. First, you want to validate their point of view. "What I hear you saying is that you have doubts that the project will be successful because we've struggled to do things like this in the past. Do I have that right?" When they answer affirmatively, you have a chance to ask them about that.

- So, what happened with that project?
- Why do you think it failed?
- How would you have done if differently?
- What do you think we could do to make it successful this time around?

When you're doing this, it's really important for you to watch your tone and body language. You don't want to give them the impression that you're patronizing them in any way, because that just puts them back on defense. Think about when you're learning a new subject that you're really excited about, and you ask questions out of a sense of wonder and curiosity—that's what you need to bring to this situation. It will give them a chance to be in charge and teach you a thing or two from their experience. Who knows, you may even discover some new insights along the way that wouldn't have come up if you hadn't probed.

If you can get them to a place of feeling like they have more control in the situation, that's a perfect time to attempt to align with them on the goal you're trying to achieve. A true work enemy is only an enemy when you have different goals and are competing with each other for the same resources and buy-in. You've now moved this person from someone who is competing against you for the attention of others to someone who's going to be amenable to coming along with you. Again, guide them with questions to keep them in the power position: "Are you saying that if we got the necessary resources and could expand the timeline, you'd be on board with this?" If they say no, then ask them what else they would need. Keep that back-and-forth going until they have nowhere else to go. And when they get to yes, you've won. Offer to follow up with them in a one-on-one conversation and schedule the meeting as soon as you can to confirm their buy-in. When you have the follow-up, make sure to lay out for them exactly what their concerns were from the previous chat so they know you heard all of their contributions. No matter what they say or what snide remark they make after that, just keep the rest of the meeting focused on the goal and how you can move forward, using questions every step of the way to cement their alignment with your goal. At the end of the meeting, throw out an open-ended question they can respond to: "Is there anything else I can do to help you or move this along?" Again, look for every opportunity to give them power, even though you're the one who's really in control. If you manage this, you will have offered them the professional validation they've been craving but probably haven't experienced in a very long time. They may not ever admit their appreciation, but you should have no doubt that it's there.

Be prepared: When you change the tenor of your interactions, your coworker is going to be incredibly skeptical of you, convinced that you have ulterior motives of some sort. That makes sense—when someone suddenly appears to be on your side out of nowhere, after months or years of a more adversarial relationship, it's natural to ask what's up. That skepticism isn't a reason to stop—it's a reason to keep going. In a 2017 interview with John Oliver, the Dalai

Lama remarked of China's hatred of him, "I practice taking others' anger, suspicion, and distrust and give them patience, tolerance, and compassion." There are times to mirror the behaviors you're seeing in others to adapt to their needs, but this is not one of those times, because when you respond to anger with anger, you just create more anger. Responding with compassion is the only way to diffuse the situation.

What if they never respond to your efforts and just continue approaching you like the enemy? So what. Their response is not your worry. Your only concern is what you're contributing to the situation, and the standard you should hold yourself to is creating a work experience that makes you happy. When you're reaching out to others, you're acting in a positive way regardless of how they receive it. When it's hard is when it really matters. You don't do it because it's the easy thing. You do it because it's the right thing to do.

WHEN WORK TURNS TOXIC

Most work enemies are relatively harmless. They may be cynical curmudgeons, but they're very manageable if they're kept in their proper sphere by maintaining your perspective around them. But there are a few types of work enemies that present a more complicated problem: The narcissists and the workplace bullies. The majority of people in the modern workplace have experienced one or both of these delightful types at some point in their career.

Workplace bullies

Bullies play the power game, levying repeated negative attacks, like criticism and humiliation, against their targets, with the specific intention of causing fear, distress, or harm. The ways bullies can attack their targets run the gamut from harassment and threats of violence, to emotional attacks (being shouted at, having allegations made against you), to job-related sabotages (persistent criticism of your work and effort, hints that you should quit, unreasonable tasks or impossible deadlines). The key is that this behavior has to be repeated—if someone does something one time, that does not meet the definition of bullying. But if it happens consistently over the course of months, you might have a bully on your hands.

Being bullied at work will make you question yourself constantly. Is this really happening? What have you done to deserve it? How can you just make it stop? Is it happening because you suck at your job? Are you an impostor? Every day you go into work will be a battle that will leave you feeling emotionally exhausted. In a situation like this, keep in mind that you are the only one who can empower yourself. There is a difference between being a victim of a workplace bully and being a target of one. A victim allows the situation to define them, using it as proof that there's no good in the world, that they can't trust anyone, and that there's no reason to fight. In the process, they build a wall that prevents them from really living and enjoying life to the fullest. A target, on the other hand, recognizes what's happening to them but is still able to move through the experience, open to the fact that there are good people in the world who aren't out to get them and that a positive outcome is possible.

If you're being targeted by a workplace bully, here's the very best advice I can give you: Do not go to HR and report them unless you are prepared to lose your job. Unless your organization has a formal process for handling these types of complaints where each is documented and investigated (hint: most don't), the chances of

them helping you are slim to none. I say this not to insult HR professionals, most of whom are very upstanding, kind people. I say
this because it's what the statistics tell me. Research shows that
eight out of ten times when workplace bullying is reported, the
organization will either do nothing to help the target, or overtly
take the side of the bully. In fact, most of the time they know exactly what's going on and take the "that's just the way they are,
learn to deal with it" approach because you're likely not the first
person the bully has targeted. I saw this directly in my own dissertation work about young professionals who were targets. I interviewed eight people about their experiences of being bullied. All
eight of them reported it to HR. In every case, the bully had targeted others and HR knew about it. Only one of them received
help. Three of them were fired after they reported it. The rest
never received the help they were looking for, most choosing to
voluntarily leave their positions for greener pastures.

Which leads us to your next step: If you want the bullying to
stop, it's time to start looking for a new job. You have to gauge
when you're ready to take this step. Think about how often you
have to work with the bully, how severe their behavior is, and how
much it is impacting your stress level. It may not seem fair that you
should have to be the one to leave the organization, but it is the
absolute best way to empower yourself in this situation. I don't care
if you've been at your job for fifteen years or fifteen minutes. It's
time to dust off the resume and start sending it out, because the
reality is that most workplace bullying ends when either the bully
or the target leaves the organization. The organization has already
shown you by sheer virtue of your bully being employed that they
are going to continue to tolerate their behavior. The very real
choice you have to make is between staying in your current

position or enjoying a work experience that does not involve being the target of a highly toxic individual. I'll take door number two.

In the meantime, mitigate your stress as best you can: Find social support in the organization, get to the gym and hit a punching bag or lift some heavy weights, and get your work-life balance under control (chapter 12 will help with that!). Most of all, have the resilience to keep your head held high and maintain your perspective. You did not cause this situation, and you do not deserve it. Allow the situation to make you question yourself, and they win. Empower yourself, and there's nothing they can do to touch you. Yes, you may have to find work elsewhere, but maintaining your sense of self is the thing that matters most and will be the thing that propels you forward.

Narcissists

The word *narcissist* gets thrown around an awful lot, but true narcissists suffer from a very real personality disorder that gives them a grandiose sense of self-importance, devoid of all empathy or guilt. They are able to create an experience in which they are the top dog at all times, no matter how much they have to stretch the truth to do it or how many people they throw under the bus. This is where the personality disorder kicks in—how they perceive reality is skewed. They're able to convince themselves that the lies they tell are true, that every conversation is about how great they are, and that they are absolutely incapable of any missteps, living in a sort of alternative reality that constantly reinforces their elevated sense of self. The disorder develops early in life and is almost impossible to officially diagnose and treat, because that involves the narcissist seeking help for it. And in their mind, they're perfect! They don't need help with a thing.

Empathy can serve you a great deal. No matter how it may seem from the outside, narcissists are not happy people. It's truly sad to live in a world where you constantly have to work to reinforce the reality that everything you do is perfect. They may be walking around outside every day like you and I, but they are in a very real mental prison that is almost impossible to escape from.

The one thing you never want to do with a narcissist is go against them in public or take the limelight away. Nothing is more important to them than maintaining their perfect self-image or being the star of the show. If they identify you as someone who's getting in their way, they will go after you relentlessly. Remember, this is not just about career success and advancement. This is deeply personal.

Should you consider leaving your job if you work with a narcissist? Maybe. It's particularly challenging when the narcissist is either your boss (they're constantly afraid of you outshining them) or your subordinate (they have no problem getting you fired so they can take your job and rise in the ranks). If you can keep their behavior in perspective and learn to play their game, they can be a lot easier to work with than a workplace bully. However, it does take a tremendous amount of energy to do so. I've had clients hire me specifically to help them with their narcissist bosses because they didn't want to leave their jobs—they made great money and had lots of perks and didn't want to give that up. So we give it a try and I give them every trick in my toolbox to help them maintain their position. Alas, they generally throw in the towel within three to six months because they're mentally exhausted and can't bring themselves to do it for a moment longer. The moral of the story is that you'll probably want to put some resumes out there just in case. Having options is never a bad thing.

MAKE IT A LEARNING EXPERIENCE

When someone leaves a job because of frustrations surrounding the difficult people they work with, they're looking for a fulfilling experience somewhere else. But what tends to happen is that they just repeat the same patterns in job after job after job. They start to think there's no point to it, that all organizations are the same, resigning themselves to a very "meh" professional experience until they hit retirement.

What they fail to realize is that there is one common denominator across all of their work experiences—them. It's not that they are provoking these situations with their colleagues, who were probably miserable before they ever showed up. Their mistake is that they are failing to learn and grow from the situations they're finding themselves in. Their environment will change their experience, but what they really need to do is change their perspective about whatever context they find themselves in. Remember, it's all about the stories you tell yourself in whatever situation you find yourself in. Frame your story well and that, on its own, will change your professional experience.

If you're unhappy in one job and you don't take a good long look in the mirror and ask yourself how you contributed to the situation, then chances are you're going to be unhappy in the next job you have. And the one after that. You'll keep repeating the same patterns until you take responsibility for the role you play.

Consider the difficult people you work with your "special

friends"—they present you with an opportunity to learn to be happy regardless of your context. The only thing you can do is come in every day and contribute to the situation in a way that reflects the experience you want to create, utilizing all the tips and tricks you've learned in this book thus far. Then, if you want to move on to your next big adventure, you will bring with you the experience to know how to maintain your power and perspective in any situation.

PART IV

refine your
path forward

This last section is a little different. It's about stepping back and looking at your life holistically, including the direction your professional experience will take from here on out.

In this section, you'll build clarity on what your true work-related passions are, learn how to make those passions a part of your day-to-day, and commit to boundaries to maintain the perfect work-life balance for you.

CHAPTER 11

Discover Career Clarity

Have the courage to follow your heart and intuition. They
somehow already know what you truly want to become.

—Steve Jobs

GOAL FOR THIS CHAPTER:

Take everything you know and rethink the direction of your career
as if you're starting again.

A friend of mine is a window washer. He's one of those people who you see hanging off the side of tall buildings,
painstakingly cleaning the outside of every pane of glass to
make sure the people inside can have a beautiful view of the world.
It's certainly not your typical professional position, or something
that most people aspire to. And because of that, it can be easy to

look at someone with that type of job and think they simply have no ambition or discipline or that they simply couldn't cut it in the "real world." If you ever met my friend outside of work, his kilt-wearing, music-festival-obsessed, quasi-hippie image would only reinforce those assumptions.

But my friend wasn't always a window washer. I met him in 2003, in my first "real" job right after I graduated from college. He was a recruiter at a military college he had also graduated from with a bachelor's in diplomacy. He wore a military uniform to work almost every day, and if he wasn't in that, it was a shirt and tie. He loved what he did, helping to guide students who wanted to travel on the same path he had gone down when he was a student. And he was really good at it, advancing through the ranks quickly and enjoying the financial rewards that came with it.

So how does one go from finding success in your stereotypical "professional" career to being a window washer? It's quite simple, really: He wasn't happy. When I asked him to rate his happiness being a window washer on a scale of one to ten, he gave it an eight. When I asked him to do the same for his job at the military college, he gave it a five, noting that the money was the only thing that kept him in it for as long as he was. He didn't have the greatest working relationship with his boss, but more than that, he simply wasn't built for office life. What looked to be a better career move from the outside was really just sucking the life out of him. So one day he quit with no plans for his next step. After a series of odd jobs—everything from running a food program in a nursing home to being a park ranger—he ended up finding happiness as a window washer. He has a boss he loves who works right beside him, and gets to work outside with stunning views in an extremely physical job that is the exact opposite of sitting behind a desk all day. Less money and prestige perhaps, but those weren't the goal. His personal happiness was the goal, perceptions of the world be damned.

Now, I'm not suggesting that you quit your job to join the ranks of the window washers of the world (unless, of course, that's what you want!). But it is certainly worth taking a step back with the self-mastery you've developed while you've been working through this book to ask yourself if the job you have makes you happy. Not content. Not financially secure. Happy.

DID YOU FOLLOW YOUR PASSION?

Have you ever felt like you just weren't doing what you were meant to be doing?

For as long as I can remember, I've been fascinated by psychology, or why people make the decisions they do. But when I got to college, besides taking a few classes here and there to fulfill requirements, I didn't study anything to do with psychology because I was raised to be "realistic," and it just seemed like a throwaway major for kids who couldn't make a commitment to something. Instead, I majored in communications, and even then I would tell people that I was doing so because I wanted to be able to get a job and make money. And I did get a job after graduation, and I did make money.

A few years later, I completed an MBA, not because business was something I was particularly passionate about but because I worked for a college at the time, could do it for free, and a master's seemed like a good thing to have that would allow me to make more money. Today, I refer to it as my superfluous degree, since I'm not sure I've used much of what I learned in my two years of study to get it. But it looked nice on paper and it did allow me to ask for more money during negotiations.

Before I knew it, I was almost thirty years old, doing marketing professionally, and making good money . . . but I wasn't happy. I presented a decent outward face to people because that was what successful people did, but I was simply not passionate about selling things. Yet our passions have a way of hanging around, even if we've done our level best to suppress them. One day, as if guided by a force larger than myself, I felt compelled to enroll in a PhD program in psychology. Now, a PhD is no joke—it is a big commitment. Still, the decision to do it was one of the easiest I've ever made in my life. It made no sense if you looked at it from the outside, but it ended up being exactly the right thing to do and facilitated my transition from a career that was "meh" to one that I wake up every day feeling truly grateful for. And today, in an utter twist of fate, I make more money practicing psychology than I ever did in marketing. I say that not to brag, but as a way of eating my own little bit of crow.

I allowed what I perceived to be the most realistic path to financial success (which I conflated with success in general) to get in the way of what I really wanted to do because I lacked the experience to know that you can make money doing almost anything, and that financial success can be a burden if you achieve it without following your passion. Unfortunately, this is a story that plays out all the time when people are making those initial decisions that start them down a particular career path.

There are many reasons why people select one career track over another, but research tells us that many are simply following the path of least resistance. They're doing what their parents want them to do, or what they see their friends doing, but it may not be part of a pragmatic strategy to get themselves in a position to do what they're most passionate about.

Said another way, they're afraid that the path they truly want to go down will be harder, so the route they perceive as easier offers them a safer, more direct path to success.

For example, you might graduate from school and apply for a lot of different entry-level positions to cast as wide a net as possible. You get no response to most of those applications, follow-up interviews to some, until finally you receive your coveted first job offer. It may not be your first choice job, or even one you're particularly excited about, but it's fine! It's a good first job that will get you some experience. Do you turn it down, waiting for the job that you're really excited about to come through? Probably not, because you're afraid that other job won't come and you've got a sure thing in front of you right now. So you take it. Even if your intention is only to be in it for a year or two before moving on to something different, life tends to get in the way of that because the path of least resistance is to stay in the lane you're in.

Sometimes it starts before you even hit the job market and you're just trying to keep the peace in your family. Say you wanted to major in English literature in college because you were passionate about a career in publishing . . . but Mom and Dad (who probably paid the tuition bill) wanted you to be a doctor. In this case, the path of least resistance was to go premed, helping you avoid the tough conversation with Mom and Dad about how medicine didn't excite you in the way that publishing did because you "knew" if you got into that conversation, they'd respond that there was no money in publishing and it was too competitive, whereas medicine provided a safe, practical career, and one that they were willing to foot the bill for. And not only did you avoid the tough conversation, but you also avoided the consequences of defying your parents' wishes by majoring in what you weren't passionate about, because you couldn't major in much of anything if the tuition bill wasn't being paid.

Of course, all of that was just a story that you created in your head because you were afraid of having the tough conversation with your parents (and perhaps you might even admit to yourself that you were afraid of what would have happened if they had supported your decision to venture into publishing if you weren't able to cut it). Regardless, you ended up going down the path you thought your parents wanted you to go down, graduating premed and going to medical school. And after you graduated, you found yourself in a similar scenario to our first example—it's much easier to stay in the lane you're in than to switch to something completely different after all that effort. In the process, you may have even convinced yourself that medicine isn't all that bad, and it is something you'd be happy doing, pushing down that part of you that dreamed of finding the next great American novel.

In the best-case scenario, you found yourself on the path that aligned with your passions early on, but that doesn't guarantee that you're still on the right path now. People make missteps in their career that can seem like great ideas at the time but unknowingly take them off course.

Throughout this book, you've already done a lot of work on yourself, and sometimes that leads to you looking at your career choices in a different way. In this chapter, we'll explore that, giving you a crystal-clear vision of where you want your career to go. You may find that what you have right now isn't far off from where your passions are, or you may discover that there's a gap. Either is perfectly fine—you'll just need a road map to follow to reach your passions and create the most fulfilling professional experience for yourself.

SELF-MASTERY EXERCISE

Think back to when you started on the path that led you to where you are today. Take out your journal and answer the following questions:

- What were you passionate about before you worried about paying bills?
- What were the circumstances?
- Who were you trying to please?
- What options did you eliminate because you were afraid?

HAPPINESS IS MORE THAN SATISFACTION

If you already had more money than you could ever spend, what would you do with your days?

When I ask this of my coaching clients, the reaction I get 95 percent of the time is an absolute "deer in the headlights" look because they haven't allowed themselves to dream about the possibilities. Then they think about it for a moment and say something to the effect of "Well, my job is fine! It's better than being a ditchdigger. Other people have it much worse than I do." Yes, that may be true . . . but when you look back on the day you retire on how you spent your life, will you be proud that the bar you reached in your career was "better than a ditchdigger"?

In 2017, the Conference Board research group declared that the majority of American workers—51 percent—were "satisfied" with their jobs. It was the first time the number had been in the majority since 2005 and was considered a positive upward trend by many of the pundits. If your child brought home a school assignment with a grade of 51 percent, would that merit hanging it on the refrigerator?

In the primary and secondary schools I attended, anything below 70 percent was considered failing.

Even the word *satisfied* is problematic because it just reinforces the "I've got it better than the ditchdigger" mentality. I'm satisfied if I get lunch at Five Guys (the vinegar for the fries alone makes it a worthwhile trip!), but that dining experience is leagues away from the euphoria I feel when I go out to a beautiful dinner at a Michelin starred restaurant. Each is good in its own way, but if I had to make a choice between the two, I'd pick fine dining every time.

Most of us aren't lucky enough to be born independently wealthy, and so working to pay the bills is a necessary part of the experience. But if your chief goals are making money, advancement, and being perceived as successful by the neighbors, this is a great way to end up in a high-level position that makes you absolutely miserable. The question is not whether you need to work, but rather how you can provide for your financial needs in a way that also makes you feel happy and fulfilled. People can make money doing almost anything—there's no reason you can't discover a position that will pay your mortgage and leave you feeling accomplished at the end of the day.

SELF-MASTERY EXERCISE

You probably go through an annual performance review at work, but have you ever taken the time to give yourself a career performance review? Do a gut check. Take out your journal and think about the following questions:

- How is your current professional experience holding up to what you want it to be?
- What are the things that are hitting the mark?

- Do you like the tasks and projects you have on your plate?
- What skills do you bring to your job that your organization is not currently taking advantage of?
- What subject matter or skills do you want to work to develop?
- What is your growth plan?

This is something you should revisit on a regular basis to make sure your career is going in the direction you'd like it to go.

KNOW WHAT YOU WANT

Let's cut right to the chase: If you could do anything for work, what would you do? Imagine an employer came to you and told you to write your own job description, putting absolutely no restrictions on it. You have carte blanche to create your ideal job from scratch. What is the thing that's going to make you truly happy?

Don't overthink this! Whether you understand it or not, you probably already know what the answer is, even if it's hidden deep in your subconscious. And remember, there are no right or wrong answers to this question. Put aside every expectation that your parents and your friends and society has of you, and remove all judgment about whether what you want is possible because almost anything is possible if you're willing to put in the work.

SELF-MASTERY EXERCISE

Take out your journal and brainstorm what your ideal job would look like:

- What is the title?
- What would you spend your days doing? What would your primary responsibilities be?

- Would it be in a traditional office, or would it be something a bit more unorthodox?
- Would you manage a team, or would you be an individual contributor?
- What would the work environment look like? Corporate, non-profit, start-up? What type of office space do you have? What's the team culture like?

Have fun with this exercise. If it doesn't excite you, then you are doing it wrong! When you're done, look over your list and read it out loud to yourself. Think about what it would be like to be in that position and how that would change your life. You should have a big smile on your face when you're done, and if that's the case, you've got to go for it.

GOING AFTER YOUR DREAM JOB

Your ideal job doesn't have to be a pipe dream—once you have a clear picture of what you're after, there's no time like the present to start looking for it. There are two main routes you can go: If your ideal job isn't far off from where you already are, you may be able to convince your employer to mold your current job to your specifications. But if the gap is wide, or if you can't find what you're looking for in your current organization, you may want to consider how you can transition your career to move in the direction of where you want to be.

You may notice that I left out a third option: Start your own company. For some people, their dream job has nothing to do with working for other people. They want the freedom that being your own boss can provide. That was very true for me—it's why I started my own company. If that's your road, there are any number of books out there that will help you to get started. However, I believe that entrepreneurship simply isn't a route for the masses, because most people enjoy the security of a steady paycheck and the benefits that come with it. So, for our purposes here, we're going to focus on jobs that are available within organizations.

CRAFTING A JOB INTERNALLY

Just because your organization doesn't have a job posting up doesn't mean the position you want is unavailable. It just means you have to champion its creation. The costs of retaining an employee are far less than losing someone and replacing them. If your current organization values you and your contribution, and wants to keep you happy, they may be open to shifting your responsibilities, or creating an entirely new position for you.

You'll bolster your case if you come up with a strong proposal. First, you want to make sure that what you're proposing is realistic with regard to the context you're working in. Where is the needs gap in your organization? How can you contribute in a way that will support its mission and goals? What type of impact will the position have? What will the ramp-up time be? When can they expect to see results? No matter what type of organization you work in, it always helps if you can trace the impact of the position you're proposing to the bottom line.

Next, write a job description. You could pull from the one you did in the earlier dream-job exercise, but do it in the style your current employer would require you to, just as if it's something that would be posted on your organization's job site. This will help people get a fuller picture of what you're proposing, and save a step later when HR requires you to write one. What are the roles and responsibilities? Will the person in this role manage a team, or will they be an individual contributor? Perhaps you envision the role starting out solo and expanding later on. That makes sense with brand-new positions—the investment in transitioning a current employee into a new individual contributor role is far less than the sticker shock of building out an entirely new team. What type of qualifications does the person in this role need? Make sure they overlap with what you bring to the table! And yes, you should absolutely have an understanding of the salary you'd want from such a position, whether it's at your current level or you're asking your organization for a raise.

Finally, account for the transition. If they're moving you into a new role, then someone has to take on your current responsibilities. Be prepared to answer the question about next steps. Do you know someone internally that could fill your current role? Would it require a full-time hire, or could your responsibilities be distributed to other team members? Would you be willing to keep some of your existing responsibilities while the position is being filled, to bridge the gap? Your goal is to make the whole thing as easy and seamless as possible.

Once you have your plan developed, you need to figure out who will make the final decision. It may be your boss, your boss's boss, a leader outside of your reporting line that you want to report into, or even the CEO. It's usually not someone in HR, though HR will probably want to be involved early on in the process, particularly if you work at a smaller organization. Your goal is to get your proposal in front of whoever the decision-maker is, but you don't want to just walk into their office and drop it on their desk. Start by testing the waters. Ask them for a meeting or a coffee and explore the topic as if it's just an idea you're exploring: "Have you ever thought about having someone in this type of role?" See what they say. If all goes well, they may even ask you if that's a position you'd be interested in before the conversation ends.

Should you let your boss know what you're doing if your proposal includes not continuing to report to them? Probably. In fact, it's probably a good idea to make them your first stop. You don't want there to be any surprises if the person you're proposing your new position to asks your boss about it or if your plan doesn't work out. And, in a best-case scenario, your boss is going to think your idea is great and will support you. However, there could also be instances where you want to go around them. For example, if you have a negative relationship with your boss, and you think your decision-maker will be able to keep the conversation you have with them confidential, it may be better to test the waters first and see if they are open to your idea. If they decide to move forward, they can help you communicate with your boss and provide you with backup. Though transparency is usually the best policy, you know your situation better than anyone else and can determine the most beneficial course of action. Simply be aware that if you choose not to include your boss in the process, there may be consequences.

Finally, when you're presenting your idea, always keep the focus on the value to the organization, and not on your own personal ambition or happiness. It's the difference between saying "here's what I want out of my career" and "here's how I can best serve the organization." Speak to it from a detached perspective and argue for the position on the merits of the role. There's nothing wrong with wanting to develop your career, but when you prioritize that, it can come across as very self-serving.

TRANSITIONING YOUR CAREER

It's wrong to say that people are afraid of change—they are afraid of the impact of the change. This is never more true than when it comes to a job or career change. What if you end up in a worse situation than you're in now? That's always a possibility. But go about transitioning your career pragmatically, and you'll set yourself up to get more of what you want, not less.

The most common form of career transition is getting a new job at a new organization. This is the route you go when the job you want is not available to you in your current company, either because it's not something that is aligned with the organization's mission or because they are unwilling to work with you to create a new role. So dust off your resume and take a look at what's out there. In most cases, there's no rush here. You still have a job and a steady paycheck—you're fine. You are under no obligation to tell your current employer you're looking, and if they find out about it, simply explain that you're exploring your options. (It could be a great chance to have a chat with them about how to morph your current role!)

There are tons of job-search resources out there, but I want to call particular attention to Liz Ryan's articles about how to craft and utilize pain letters. One of the most frustrating aspects of the job search is that you send out a ton of resumes and never get a call back. That's because most organizations use software to sift through all the resumes that come in, so a real-life human being might not ever see yours. Pain letters are a way around the automated system. Here's how it works:

- You identify a job you want to apply for. Go research the employer and figure out what problems the open position will help them to solve. Every open position that every organization has solves a problem or fills a gap. Otherwise, they wouldn't be hiring for it. The roles and responsibilities of the job should give you a good idea of what that is.

- Next, figure out how the problem they need help with aligns with a problem you can help them solve based on your experience and skills. It doesn't have to be an exact match with what you're doing right now, but there should be some overlap.

- Do some research and figure out who the hiring manager is for the position. This is not an HR title! This is the person that the position would report to. If you're applying for a marketing manager role, you're probably looking for the marketing director. Use LinkedIn to figure out exactly who that person is. You may even be able to ask the company's HR department. Sometimes they'll give out that information and sometimes they won't, but it's worth a try!

- Once you have all that information, craft a very brief letter to the hiring manager that discusses the problem you think they want to solve and gives an example of when you've solved a problem like it before. The shorter this letter is, the better! You're just trying to get their attention. If you Google "Liz Ryan pain letters," you'll find lots of examples of how this works.

- Print out the letter, staple it to your resume, and send it to the hiring manager snail-mail style.

Doing it this way will ensure your resume gets in front of the person making the hiring decision, regardless of what the algorithm says. For good measure, apply via the official website too. Some companies will not consider a hire until they are in the official system. That way, if your potential new boss checks in with HR and asks them to bring you in for an interview, you'll already be on the list of applicants.

If you're planning on making a complete departure from your current profession to an entirely new realm, understand that this will take time. You may have to go back to school and get new certifications, and you will need to convince someone to give you that first opportunity. Don't let that scare you away—it's perfectly achievable. It just might take some work. It took me seven years to fully transition from being a marketing professional to the work I do today, and I don't regret a single moment of it. Once you meet your goal, you won't look back and think, "What a waste of time!" You'll say, "I wish I had done it sooner."

SELF-MASTERY EXERCISE

If you're seeking a full career transition, take out your journal and start brainstorming a list of all the steps you'll need to take to make it a reality. What skills, knowledge, or certifications/degrees will you need? What is the typical career path someone in that type of position takes? Would you need to start out at a lower level, both in terms of seniority and also salary, and work your way up? Don't let any of these steps intimidate you—you just need to have a jumping-off point. Approach it from your beautifully detached perspective. It's not good or bad. It just is.

Not sure where to start? A great first step might be to reach out to someone in your network who does what you want to do and ask if you can take them out for a cup of coffee or schedule a phone call with them. Ask them how they got to where they are. If you don't know someone directly, just reach out to your network and see if you can find a friend of a friend. You might be surprised at how easy it is to make a connection. And who knows! They could end up being the person who mentors you on your journey.

Remember, the hardest part of making a full career transition is simply taking the first step. Once you do it, you'll gain momentum and continuing to move forward will be a piece of cake.

KNOW YOU'RE WORTH IT

In truth, the thing that holds most people back from going after their dream job is that they don't think they deserve it. They will come up with every excuse in the book—it's too hard to find, my resume isn't updated, I've only been in my job for a year, I don't want to move, I don't want to start over again, etc. I could go on and on, because I've heard them all from people I've coached. When we drill below the surface, what almost always comes up is a sense that they are not worthy. A dream job might be achievable for other people, but not for them.

Look at a picture of newborns and ask yourself if any of them is more worthy of a beautiful life than any other. Clearly, the answer is no. Just because you grow up and have experiences, successes, and failures does not mean that your worth is diminished. When you remove the judgments of good and bad, we're all just people, trying to do the best we can every single day. There is not a single person on this earth that is more deserving of their dream job than you. There are simply people who choose to go after what they want and people who don't. You decide which group you're in. Even if you've made one choice in the past, you can always make a different choice today. Every moment is a chance to begin again.

CHAPTER 12

Find Your Balance

True life is lived when tiny changes occur.

—Leo Tolstoy

GOAL FOR THIS CHAPTER:

Set boundaries that support the full life you want to lead, in and outside of work.

hear it from clients all the time:

"I don't have balance."

"My organization expects me to work all the time."

"I can never turn off."

So we do a little experiment. First, I ask them to stop checking their work email at night. This usually causes a bit of anxiety— what if it's an emergency?! But eventually they give it a shot. Once they get home, their work email gets shut off. I even convince some of them to take their work email off their cell phone, so that if they leave their laptop at work, they won't be able to cheat and check it anyway.

Lo and behold, they do it for a few days and nothing bad happens. They find that any emails they get after hours can just as easily be answered the next morning as they can while they are at home, and no buildings burn down overnight as a result of a message not being immediately returned. Soon the number of emails they get at night starts to go down because they aren't engaging in any after-hours back-and-forth.

With one successful experiment under our belts, we move to the next level: For one week, I ask them to commit to a normal, forty-hour work schedule, or as close as they can get to it given the culture of their organization. That means they get in at nine a.m., leave at five p.m., and do not do work before or after hours unless it is an absolute emergency. If a project doesn't get done, they don't stay late to finish it—they simply pick up where they left off the next day. Again, that anxiety that popped up when I asked them to stop checking their email at night creeps back in, but ultimately we agree that it's just one week—if it doesn't work, they can go right back to working all the extra hours they want. At the end of the week, we evaluate how it went . . . and nothing bad has happened. In fact, most of the time their boss and their coworkers didn't even notice that they aren't working overtime, which can make my clients mad! They discover they're putting in all this extra effort and people can't even tell the difference when they stop. As a bonus, they discover that they create more urgency and efficiency for themselves at work, since they know they're restricted in the amount of hours they're working, and use their time more wisely and efficiently. That means they get the same amount of work done in fewer hours because they are more focused on the things that matter. Suddenly, these few simple changes have them viewing the problem of work-life balance differently—they didn't have to change their organization, or their boss, or their coworkers, or even their workload. They just had to adjust how they were doing things, and take responsibility for creating the type of experience they want.

YOUR WORK-LIFE BALANCE IS YOUR RESPONSIBILITY

Work-life balance is one of the top predictors of job satisfaction. That means that if you want your professional experience to be amazing, you must have a life outside of work that supports it. Try as we might to build a big wall between them, your professional life and your personal life are not separate from each other—the two are intrinsically entwined. Consider it a package deal—your work experience impacts your personal life, and vice versa. If you have a bad morning at home, you're going to be in a cranky mood before you ever get to the office . . . and if you have a bad day of work, that will follow you home at night, leaving you too mentally drained to enjoy time with your family.

Here's the hard truth: If you feel that your work-life balance is out of whack, more times than not, that is your responsibility. It's easy to blame everyone and everything around you, but your boss is usually not holding a gun to your head and forcing you to work long hours, nights, and weekends, or to not take your vacation days. Those are choices you are making, having convinced yourself that your job requires you to do it when that may not be the case. Owning those choices is the only way to change the experience you're having.

BALANCE IS INDIVIDUAL

The word *balance* is a bit tricky because it implies an even distribution—you have your work on one side of the scale and your life on the other side, and you only have balance if the two sides are even. But when it's applied in the real world, what works beautifully for one person will be an absolute disaster for another person. There is no such thing as a perfect formula for work-life balance that suits everyone. As we move through the process of discovering what it looks like for you, resist the urge to compare your version of it to anyone else's. What works for your spouse or your brother or your best friend may or may not be perfect for you.

What's more, your personal definition of work-life balance will evolve as you get older and your life circumstances change. When you're a single young professional, your idea of balance may entail working sixty to eighty hours a week and enjoying the hustle of trying to get ahead, which is very different from when you're in your forties, married, with a few kids at home. Giving up a routine that you've been doing for years can be difficult, but it's okay to admit that what worked for you at one point in your life may no longer suit your current needs.

Figuring out what your definition of balance is in the present may require a bit of experimentation, but your goal is simple: You want your daily routine to support your feeling great. What makes you feel amazing? What makes you feel physically good and men-tally sharp, and gives you the energy you need to easily make it through the day from the moment you get up until your head hits the pillow at night?

SELF-MASTERY EXERCISE

To start figuring out what work-life balance means to you, let's create a vision of what your ideal experience looks like across a variety of areas. Don't rush through this exercise—go someplace quiet and comfortable, take out your journal, and give yourself time to consider each area as though you had no restrictions. Remember, there are no right or wrong answers here—just write the first thing that comes to mind. When in doubt, ask yourself what makes you feel really good.

- **Physical health:** Do you want to work out regularly? How many days a week? What types of workouts make you feel great? What type of diet works best for you? What types of food should you eat, and what do you want to avoid? How much sleep should you get?
- **Friends/family:** What do you want your relationships to look like? How large do you want your circle to be? How much interaction do you want to have? You may enjoy extended networks with lots of friends and contacts, or you may prefer just a few close relationships.
- **Your significant other:** Are you in a relationship with a partner? Do you want to be? (Hint: Not everyone does, and that's okay!) What do you want that relationship to look like so that your personal needs are fulfilled?
- **Your professional career:** Do you enjoy the hustle of an extended week, or is it important to you to keep things to forty hours? Now, before you answer, really take a moment to consider this question. If you love your job and are passionate about your work, then your definition of balance may include a workweek that is fifty, sixty, or eighty-plus hours. That's just as okay as someone who wants to limit their time in the office to forty hours.
- **Leisure/fun:** What do you do when you're not working? What would you like to be doing? What hobbies are important for you to start/restart/maintain? How do you like spending your time on the

weekend, when things like household chores and errands aren't filling up your schedule? These are things that you do just for yourself—not because your partner or your best friend likes them.

- **Spirituality:** What role does faith or a spiritual practice play in your life? What role do you want it to play? If you don't have an answer for this question, it's okay—this plays a more important role for some people than it does for others.

- **Anything else?** Is there a topic that's important to you that wasn't covered in any of these areas? Make sure it's on the list!

SET YOUR PRIORITIES

With a better sense of your targets in each of the important areas of your life, it's time to home in on the top things that are really important. Look at the list you've made and identify your top three priorities. Of all the elements you just brainstormed, what are your absolute nonnegotiables? You could take a highlighter to them or circle them in a different color pen, but make sure you understand them in order of importance—you don't want to work to fit in your #3 priority on your schedule before you get to the thing that's at the top of the list.

The reason we're focusing on three to start with is that it makes the goal achievable. That's not to say that you can't integrate more of the elements from your list later on, once you've got your schedule under control. But when you try to do too much too soon, you're just setting yourself up for burnout or failure. Baby step into your new routine, changing it up a little bit at a time until you acclimate to the new reality. Then you can continue to make other tweaks.

SELF-MASTERY EXERCISE

Once you've identified your top three priorities, write down each on a new page in your journal, with some space between them. You're going to use that extra space to discuss why the priority is important to you. Your page should look a little something like this.

- My #1 priority is:
    - The reason this is important is:
    - The impact of making this a part of my day will be:
- My #2 priority is:
    - The reason this is important is:
    - The impact of making this a part of my day will be:
- My #3 priority is:
    - The reason this is important is:
    - The impact of making this a part of my day will be:

In the process of thinking your reasons and the impacts through, you may discover that one of the things you identified as your top priorities isn't really all that important, and that something you left off the list should have been included. Be open to those realizations and start again.

ACHIEVING WORK-LIFE BALANCE REQUIRES SACRIFICE

I have a confession to make: I love the idea of working out, but I have such a struggle making the trip to the gym on a regular basis. It's not that I can't make the time—it's just that I have a really bad habit of choosing to veg on Netflix and knit over getting a workout in. Once I sit down on my living room couch after a day of work, it's all over. I'm not getting up. Now, if I have made the decision that Netflix and knitting is the most important thing to me, that's fine. But if I've committed to my physical health being a priority, then I have to suck it up, sacrifice my couch time, and get to the gym.

This is why understanding the reasons for your top priorities is so important—you're probably going to have to change habits in order to give your priorities a place in your schedule. It's easy to think about this conceptually—there's a limited number of hours in the day. That means when you're adding new elements to your schedule, you're going to have to take things away. But when you get into your day-to-day, it's going to be easy to fall into your old way of doing things. When the going gets tough, you want to re-mind yourself why you're making the sacrifices you are and what you'll get in return. This is about honoring the commitment you've made to yourself, knowing that doing so will lead you to a more fulfilling experience.

SELF-MASTERY EXERCISE

You know what you want to do. You know why you're doing it. Now you just have to come up with the how. It's time to plan your ideal schedule for the upcoming week.

Get a daily planner that allows you to look at a full week, with space for you to plan each hour in the day. You could print something off the internet, get a calendar at the store, or use a calendar app on your computer. Anything will work, as long as you can account for every hour of every day. Fill in the following elements, in order:

- The hours you have to be at work for your regular schedule, with no overtime. Don't plan to go in early or stay late.
- The hours you need to sleep to make sure you're getting enough rest—the times you want to go to bed at night and wake up in the morning.

- What you need to do to honor your priorities, in order of importance. How will you fit them in? When will you do what? You don't need to do every one of your priorities every day (the gym, for example, could be a three-days-a-week thing). You just need to make sure you're accounting for them as a consistent part of your routine.
- Any of the remaining space is fair game for you to use as you will. But be careful—just because you can fill those spaces with things to do doesn't mean you should. Try to do too much and you could burn yourself out.

Give your ideal schedule a try for a week, really committing to making it happen as you've planned it unless an emergency comes up. You can do anything for a week! Keep track of how things work and how often you achieve everything you planned for, and reevaluate it at the end of the week. What worked? What didn't? Is it reasonable or did you overschedule yourself? How does the new routine make you feel? Make tweaks based on your experience. This type of check-in should occur on an ongoing basis to make sure your schedule is always supporting the lifestyle you want. But above all else, remind yourself that you've set the priorities you have for a reason. Unless you're changing them because you've discovered that something else is more important to you, be very disciplined about keeping them as a part of your regular schedule.

BRING IT BACK TO WORK

Finally, let's bring this back around to work. When you're committing to working a schedule that includes as little overtime as possible, it's important that you make good use of the time you have in the office. Making small tweaks to your day can make a big difference in your efficiency, allowing you to do more in less time.

Learn to say no

One of the reasons that work-life balance can get so out of whack is because you're taking on responsibilities and tasks that don't contribute to your personal goals or help you hit your performance targets. Changing that is going to require you to do something uncomfortable—you're going to have to say no. If saying yes to something leaves you frustrated, stressed out, and off task, then you've said yes to the wrong thing.

So often it's those last-minute things that pop up that disrupt your workflow. But remember that poor planning on someone else's part does not constitute an emergency for you unless you allow it to. It can help to say no while offering a flexible, reasonable option. "I can't do it today, but I can get it over to you by the end of the day tomorrow. Will that work?" If they continue to push, hold your ground. If you've been one of those people who takes on last-minute tasks willingly in the past, you've taught them to expect that from you. In honoring your boundaries, you're teaching them a new way of working with you, which can take a bit of adjustment. Ignore the little voice in your head telling you that it's just this one time, because one time leads to more. It's like learning a new habit—it requires consistent effort. Don't fight with them or get into a debate about it—you still need to maintain a positive working relationship. Just stick to your guns and reiterate that you'll be happy to get it to them tomorrow.

A tactic that can really help you to say no is to simply block off work time on your calendar for you to focus on tasks you need to accomplish. What happens when you have an open space on your calendar? Someone schedules you for a meeting, every single time. Before you know it, your day is full of meetings and you have no time for work. Blocking your calendar allows you to make the time. Start small—try blocking an hour every single day that is your focused desk time. If you have an office door, this is the time to shut it to send the message to passersby that you are unavailable. If you work at a cubicle, you could have some fun with it and hang a sign at your desk that says "Closed for business." Wearing a large pair of headphones that people can easily see (i.e., not earbuds) can also send the same message, even if you don't have any music playing. And if someone asks you if they can schedule you for a meeting during your blocked time, it's a perfect chance to practice saying "no!"

Turn off your email

Of all the changes I suggest people make, this is the one I get the most pushback on. It's time to stop the email insanity. You have to turn off your email. Not just after hours—during the day. If you're like many people, you've gotten yourself into the awful habit of answering most emails the minute they come in. Every time you do that, you're taking your attention off whatever project you're working on and are now focused on crafting the perfect message. It doesn't allow you to create a sense of flow with your work, where you're fully immersed in what you're doing and the hours seem to fly by like minutes. Flow is when you reach your maximum state of productivity.

Many people in the modern workforce don't remember a time before email, but I can assure you that time did exist and people

were still able to get things done. I'm not arguing that you ditch
email entirely, but you can find a balance between being respon-
sive to email and allowing it to take control of your day. Give this
a try: For the first forty-five minutes of every hour, turn your
email completely off and focus on the tasks in front of you. Then,
for the last fifteen minutes, open it back up and respond to what
you need to. That way, you're still answering messages in a timely
manner, but you're also allowing yourself time to focus. If there's
an emergency, someone will come and find you, or at least call you
on the phone (probably to ask why you haven't responded to their
email yet!).

More broadly, this is about putting an end to constant multitasking. Multitasking can make you feel like you're accomplishing
more, but research has shown time and time again that it's causing
you to get less done (and what you do get done is often of lesser
quality). When your email is open on your desktop every moment
of every day, you're in constant danger of getting a notification or
having a sound go off to alert you to a new message, which takes
your focus away from what you're working on. That means your
brain is switching from one task to another.

Pass on the vent sessions

You know what I'm talking about—those stolen moments in the
office kitchen, chats behind a closed office door about how much
you disagree with a decision, catching up on the latest rumors and
gossip with the office manager. It's just a bit of harmless chatter and
complaining among friends . . . How much time could it really
take? All those conversations add up and, even if it's only an hour
or two every single week, that's still an hour or two that could be

spent serving your goals instead so you don't have to work after hours.

But beyond the time commitment, all those conversations about things you don't like at work or speculations about what decisions the CEO might make in the future are just not good for your headspace. It keeps you focused on the things you don't like instead of on all the things you've got going for you and what you need to accomplish. Not to mention that anything you say has the chance of becoming gossip, and can and will be used against you! It's all about what serves your personal goals—anything that does not enhance your experience has got to take a back seat.

KEEP THE END GOAL CONSTANTLY IN MIND

When it comes to building and maintaining a positive work-life balance, it's about the choices you make every day. It's an ongoing process of mindfully committing to what will make you stronger, more efficient, and happier. The better you do it, the easier every challenging element of your workday becomes. That's the payoff. But when you first start, you've got a bunch of old habits to break. If you have a bad day, don't judge yourself too harshly. The moment it happens, it's already in the past—there's nothing you can do about it. Just get back to your plan and keep moving forward as if you're still on target, meeting as many of your priorities for the rest of the day as you can. And when you wake up tomorrow, you've got a whole new day to try again.

Closing Thoughts:
It's Time to Commit

A few weeks after I completed the initial manuscript for this book, I attended a workshop led by Dr. Joe Dispenza, a lecturer and researcher who teaches the benefits of meditation from a neuroscience perspective. I hadn't been a student of his prior to that—I just signed up for the workshop on a whim after a wine-filled dinner with a friend who insisted that I simply must go. The timing of that leap of faith was serendipitous to this project, because a focal point of Dr. Joe's work stresses the commitment required to make true, lasting change in your life, emphasizing that your desire for change has got to be greater than your addiction to your current state. That's what makes change so difficult.

People get addicted to all sorts of things that aren't good for them: smoking, food, drinking, drugs, sex, toxic relationships, etc. . . . Rarely do we think about being addicted to frustrating and unfulfilling work experiences. Instead, we think of it as an unchangeable fact—work is work, something that is outside of our ability to control. This book provides a counterpoint and a strategy for change, but it doesn't give you the most critical component: The will to make it happen. Only you can provide that last piece.

Why would you get addicted to a less-than-ideal work experience? Simple: When we experience something for an extended period, that becomes our "normal," and anything outside of that comfort zone makes us uneasy. And when something feels uncomfortable, we find a way to restore stasis, even if that requires embracing things that aren't for our greatest good. If you pick up Dr. Joe's book *Breaking the Habit of Being Yourself* (which I highly recommend as your next read!), he'll explain the science of why this is occurring. But for now, here's the short version: When you're under emotional stress, your brain produces a batch of hormones that feed into the body to make it physically feel the stress you're experiencing. Over time, your body gets addicted to it, just like it does to smoking. Take the emotional stress away, and your body starts to go through withdrawal, demanding its fix of chemicals from the brain. Thus, you start subconsciously creating stories to create stressful situations that aren't real to feed your addiction. Spend years, or decades, doing this and that becomes a hard habit to break.

I see it all the time, both in my professional practice and my personal relationships: People love to complain about work! The coworkers they hate, the executives who are out of touch, the deadlines others are constantly missing, not making enough money, having no work-life balance. If the problem they complained about yesterday is solved, they'll find a new thing to complain about to fill the void. And if you offer them help in the form of a book like this, or a class, or a coaching program to help them create a better experience, they'll say, "Oh, that's a great idea!" and then never take you up on it because their addiction to their current situation is greater than their desire to change. There's nothing that can help them until they make the choice to reverse the situation.

So, you've reached the end of the book. You've got twelve chapters' worth of ideas and strategies that you can start using today. The question then becomes, is your desire for change greater than your attachment to your current circumstances?

I'm living proof that making this change is possible. But as I was also quick to say way back in chapter 1, it's incredibly hard to do. You'll have good days and bad days, days when you'll be completely zen and days when you question why you're even bothering. Your goal shouldn't be perfection. It should be making the decision to show up when you're still lying in bed each morning, knowing that it will be a little easier with each successful day you have. Show up enough and you'll create a new comfort zone, where your addiction will be to feeling productive, accomplished, and happy, and anything that doesn't measure up to that standard is the thing that feels uncomfortable.

ACKNOWLEDGMENTS

When I first started working with my coach, Joshua MacGuire, a few years ago, I told him I wanted to write a book. At that time, it was a pipe dream at best—I had a ton of ideas but no real direction. I never would have predicted that this would be the final result. Since I finished the manuscript, I've joked with him that he's actually the person who wrote this book, since so many of my ideas were refined and clarified during our weekly meetings. He was with me every step of the way, from helping me sift through all my ideas and developing the outline, to when I signed my deal with the publisher, to listening to me complain and freak out when I didn't think I would meet my deadline, and even taking his red pen to every bit of copy I wrote before I sent it over to my editor. Joshua, you have changed my life in so many ways that I never would have predicted when I decided to sign up for a month of coaching with you on a whim. Thank you for being a constant source of support and encouragement. Your faith in me gives me the strength to go after things that seem impossible, and my experience is so much better for it.

There are, of course, others who had a direct hand in making this book possible. When I was approached by a few publishers after speaking at South by Southwest, I reached out to my literary agent, Giles Anderson, with a partially put-together book proposal, declaring that I had no idea about traditional publishing and I needed help. Ever the calm, rational influence, Giles provided a lot of validation for my ideas and guided me expertly through the process of developing them into a thoughtful proposal. He brought it to Joanna Ng and the fine folks at TarcherPerigee, who are responsible for you reading it now. Thank you, Giles and Joanna, for your guidance and for making the process seem so deceptively easy.

In chapter 2, I tell the story of losing a job in a particularly brutal way that left me depressed and questioning my abilities and own self-worth for a while afterward. What I didn't mention were the people who got me through that experience. Of course, my husband was there (as he always is!) but who really got me through that awful experience were The Kittens, a wonderful group I met through the conference circuit whom I had kept in touch with. At a time in my life when I felt like so many people I trusted were turning their backs on me, this group of friends rallied around me and helped me not to feel so alone. It's hard to express without choking up, but I don't know if any of them really understands how much that simple act meant to me. Since then, I've had some of my most wonderful (and memorable!) experiences with them. You all know who you are, and you all have a very special place in my heart.

Finally, I would be remiss if I didn't thank my husband, Victor, a source of unwavering support and encouragement. I can't imagine many husbands putting up with the things that he does, from taking a chance on my business when we didn't have a ton of money in the bank, to my solo travel schedule while he stays home and takes care of our dogs. Victor, I hope you know how much I love you and appreciate everything you do for me. None of this would be possible with you.

ABOUT THE AUTHOR

Karlyn Borysenko, MBA, PhD, is an organizational psychologist, consultant, and executive coach. As the creator and owner of Zen Workplace, she helps individuals find greater happiness and fulfillment in their professional lives, and helps organizations around the world to create positive employee experiences that drive productivity. Her approach is grounded in organizational and positive psychology and draws on mindfulness techniques.